The Virtual Entrepreneur

Electronic Commerce in the 21st Century

John W. Jones, Ph.D.
Industrial-Organizational Psychologist

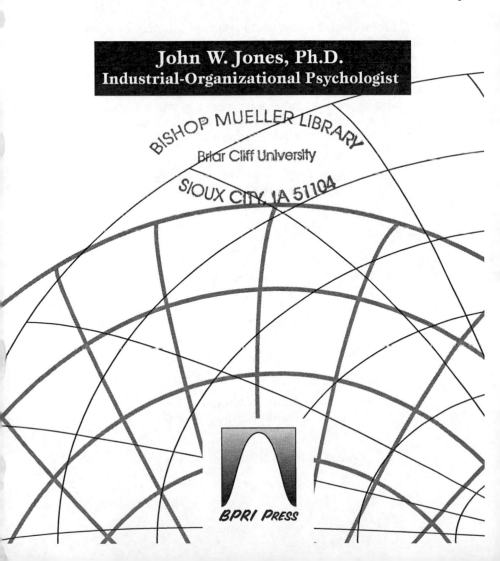

BPRI PRESS

Business Psychology Research Institute
824 East Rand Road, Suite 274
Arlington Heights, IL 60004
URL: WWW.BPRI.COM
Phone: 847/255-5481
Fax: 847/255-3480
E-Mail: BPRI2000@AOL.COM

Designed by Kim Allen-Hohman

ISBN 0-9668417-1-9

Library of Congress
Catalog Card Number: 98-96755

Printed in the United States of America

Printed by Cedar Publishing, Cedar Rapids, Iowa

ACKNOWLEDGEMENTS

I am thankful to pioneering entrepreneurs like Paul Farrow and Ruth Owades who were among the first small business owners to use the virtual organization as a major source of competitive advantage. I tried to showcase their innovative strategies as I laid the foundation for a five-step model of virtual entrepreneurship. Without their risk taking, this book could not have been written. Moreover, the future growth of the global economy, especially in terms of job creation, rests in part with virtual entrepreneurs like Farrow and Owades.

I am also appreciative of the major innovators in the computer hardware, software, and services industry that helped to inspire this work. The list of dignitaries includes Intel, Microsoft, America Online, and Dell Computer, to name a few. Although **The Virtual Entrepreneur** is a business fable, I did mention many of these innovators in the context of this business story. I also want to express my appreciation to the on-line virtual enterprises that I mentioned in this book, including Virtual Vineyards, 1-800-Flowers, and eSchwab. Their Web sites are truly inspirational!

Finally, I am thankful to my virtual team. This group of talented individuals helped me move from a concept to a tangible product in record time. The core team members included William Greenleaf, Kim Allen-Hohman, Gladys Hawkins, and Lisa Griegel. Each of these team members focused on their core competencies, thus ensuring that the final product exceeded the sum of their individual contributions.

I hope that readers will take the practical knowledge presented in this book and use it when they decide to become virtual entrepreneurs. I am confident that readers will someday prosper from using what they have learned from reading **The Virtual Entrepreneur**. Small business owners and managers who have the courage to continually re-invent themselves by learning new management strategies and practices will surely become the most successful entrepreneurs in the 21st century.

John W. Jones, Ph.D.

January, 1999

Contents

PROLOGUE:
"VIRTUAL ENTREPRENEURSHIP"

Once upon a time, there was an aspiring young entrepreneur named Steve Cole. Steve passionately wanted to leave his nine-to-five job and become a successful small business owner.

Through discipline and hard work, Steve saved $50,000 to invest in his own start-up company. Before taking the plunge, however, he wanted to learn the most important secrets of managing a small business. He did not want to rely on outdated or potentially irrelevant approaches to management that would jeopardize his entrepreneurial dreams.

Steve began looking for a seasoned entrepreneur who could teach him how to become an effective, contemporary manager. Most of the managers he initially contacted had received their MBAs from leading business schools. They knew a lot about finance, accounting, and rigorous business controls in large companies, but they knew little about entrepreneurship and how to successfully launch and steer a small business venture. They also knew little about contemporary management strategies such as visionary leadership, high-speed management, and electronic commerce.

Instead, most of the MBA managers were too bureaucratic and preferred an overly analytical and number-crunching approach to business. Steve sensed a serious mismatch between the typical MBA approach and the cutting-edge entrepreneurial strategies he needed to learn in order to launch and manage his own small business.

In short, he needed a visionary mentor.

Then Steve met The Virtual Entrepreneur, and his adventure began!

———————

There is a definite paradigm shift under way in which larger, vertically structured, overly bureaucratic and slower-responding companies are being outperformed, and at times supplanted by, smaller and swifter "virtual companies."

A virtual company is best described as a network of experts who band together, sometimes on a time-limited basis, to quickly and profitably design, produce, and market a product or service for a targeted group of customers. Although the virtual company may appear as a single entity to customers, the individual companies typically retain their separate legal identities. Virtual companies are not only revolutionizing the business world, they are also forming the management model for the 21st century.

The new management paradigm, which Steve Cole will come to know as "virtual entrepreneurship," is still in its infancy, but it will continue to grow in relevancy and sophistication. Virtuality offers entrepreneurs an opportunity to quickly leverage and stretch their resources in order to gain rapid access to new markets. Virtual entrepreneurs use strategic alliances and electronic commerce to instantly expand their own organizations' capabilities and areas of expertise. They do not hesitate to reinvent their virtual companies once particular marketing opportunities shrink or even vanish.

Over the course of this "business novel," the Virtual Entrepreneur shares with Steve his unique philosophy of contemporary entrepreneurship, along with five guiding principles that helped him successfully conceptualize, launch, and manage his virtual company, Night Vision Sports.

Armed with these lessons, Steve is eager to meet the challenge of establishing his own virtual enterprise.

NETWORKING WITH EXPERTS

Steve Cole majored in business as an undergraduate, and his dream was to someday run his own business. Unfortunately, his university did not offer a program in entrepreneurial studies.

After graduating, Steve prided himself on diligently studying magazine articles and books on how to effectively start and manage a small business. He also attended business seminars and continuing education classes on the topic, and he even used his desktop computer to access management development conferences and forums that were available on the Internet. Unfortunately, all of the material he studied seemed outdated and boring.

One evening Steve found himself sitting in front of his Intel-powered desktop computer. His home office was illuminated by both his 3-D screen saver and his green halogen desk lamp. It was nearly 10:00, but Steve was not quite ready to call it a day. He was taking a few days of vacation from his job, and he wanted to make full use of them.

The screen saver flicked off as Steve logged onto America Online. He wanted to retrieve some recent case studies on small business success stories that were available on the World Wide Web. He felt a sense of excitement as he heard his high-speed modem dialing into the online service, and he saw the phrase *Connected to Service* flash on his computer screen.

Steve quickly accessed a Web site entitled *The Entrepreneur's Network.* He used his smart mouse to click his way through opening menu screens that presented him with several options. He paused, trying to decide whether to review business news stories of the day or participate in an online forum in which he could send electronic messages back and forth with both aspiring and successful entrepreneurs.

I'll interact electronically with some entrepreneurs who might be able to help me with my search, Steve decided. He clicked onto a menu option that allowed him to type in a code name to use when chatting online. *I'll call myself The Searcher. Maybe this code name will catch the attention of some helpful online entrepreneurs who will have the answers I need!*

Steve soon found himself in a chat room where five entrepreneurs were already communicating online. He was prompted to type in a question or statement so that the logged-in entrepreneurs could choose to respond. Steve thought for a moment, then typed in his first electronic message:

> I am searching for a contemporary model of small business management that will give me a competitive advantage when I launch my first entrepreneurial company. I've heard everything the scholarly MBAs have to say about traditional management. Unfortunately, I think many of their points are irrelevant to my entrepreneurial dreams. Besides, traditional companies and their managers have trouble mobilizing their resources fast enough to seize and capitalize on fleeting yet potentially lucrative market opportunities. Can anyone enlighten me?

He took a moment to review the crisp white lettering against the blue screen on his high-resolution monitor, then gave himself a satisfied nod and hit the *Enter* key to post it. He knew he would have a brief wait before any online entrepreneurs might take the time to read his message and reply. He yawned and decided to get a piping hot cup of Columbian coffee from his kitchen.

Upon returning to his computer, he was pleasantly surprised to see that a reply had already been posted in the chat room dialogue box. Steve was in awe of the lightning quick responses that characterize the information age! He could hardly wait to see who had responded so quickly to his challenge.

Steve immediately clicked onto an icon that allowed him to print out a summary of the electronic dialogue that was occurring in the chat room. He'd had a hard day at work and was feeling a little tired, so he decided to print the dialogue summary and read it while resting on his couch. The coffee was soothing to drink, but it had not given him the lift he was hoping for.

Steve clicked on the *Print* button and heard his color laser printer kick into action. After a few seconds, his printer delivered the printout. Steve began to study it as he stretched out on the couch. His eyes ran down over the lines until he found the message addressed to him. He stared intently at the following five words:

Have you explored virtual entrepreneurship?

Steve had never heard of that style of management, yet intuitively he felt confident that he had just received a very important message. The message followed the name *The Virtual Entrepreneur.* More importantly, the respondent provided an electronic mailing address for future online dialogues away from the chat room.

Steve thought about writing back immediately to the Virtual Entrepreneur, but decided to wait until morning, when he would be feeling more energetic and alert.

He got up from the couch to return to his workstation. He went through the shut-down routine for his computer, then turned off the surge-protected power strip. Both his computer and printer fell silent, and his 17-inch monitor went dark.

Steve headed for bed.

Little did he know that he had just networked with a contemporary entrepreneur who would forever change the way he would view small business management.

AN ONLINE DIALOGUE

Steve Cole awoke early the next day. As was his custom each morning, he had a light breakfast of orange juice and granola cereal, then went to the treadmill in his spare bedroom. After a few minutes of warm-up stretching exercises, he set the treadmill's electronic controls for a twenty-minute workout at a brisk walk. Following the programmed setting, the surface of the treadmill was level at first, but the front lifted slightly every few minutes to simulate a steepening incline.

By the end of the twenty minutes, Steve had gotten a good aerobic workout. Since he worked in an office all day, he knew that physical exercise was important to help him keep fit. Walking or jogging on the treadmill wasn't particularly exciting, but it was convenient because it provided a safe environment and allowed him to exercise rain or shine.

I just wish somebody could figure out a way to make it less boring! thought Steve as he headed for the shower.

Steve was eager to follow up on the message he'd gotten from the Virtual Entrepreneur the night before. After a quick shower and change of clothes, he grabbed some coffee from the kitchen, sat down at his workstation, and logged onto his computer. He skillfully navigated his way to his favorite online Web site, *The Entrepreneur's Network.* The opening menu appeared, and he clicked on the button labeled *Send an E-mail.* Steve quickly typed in the following message on the blank blue screen:

Thanks for the tip on virtual entrepreneurship. My answer to your question is "no," I have never been informed about any form of virtual management. None of the MBAs I spoke with brought up this approach either. I must admit that I am very interested in learning more about this contemporary management concept, and I am hoping we can have an online dialogue as soon as possible. Respectfully, The Searcher.

Steve spell-checked and saved his message, then scrolled down the list of online names and E-mail addresses in the site address file. He quickly located and selected the Virtual Entrepreneur's E-mail address, then clicked on the *Send* button located on the menu screen. He felt assured that his E-mail would instantaneously find its target.

Before leaving to run some errands, Steve navigated his way through the daily *Headline News* section of his online service. He quickly scanned the day's news stories, checked the weather forecast, then logged off the service. Since he knew he would be using the computer later, he decided not to shut it down. Steve hoped to receive a reply from the Virtual Entrepreneur by that evening. His feelings of anticipation and excitement were already starting to grow!

———————

After running his errands, Steve returned to his home office at around 2:00 in the afternoon, and immediately logged onto his online service. He didn't seriously expect to find a message from the Virtual Entrepreneur so soon, but his hopes grew when he saw the blinking icon labeled *You Have Mail.*

Steve eagerly retrieved his E-mail and read the following on-screen message from the Virtual Entrepreneur:

I am pleased to see that you are so skilled at online navigating. The Entrepreneur's Network is one of my favorite cyberspace communities. In fact, I know a number of high-tech virtual entrepreneurs who have prospered nicely by combining their computer savvy with an ability to skillfully navigate their way around the emerging electronic villages and information highways.

Steve studied the message for a moment, pleased to see that the Virtual Entrepreneur seemed comfortable using terminology such as "online navigating," "cyberspace communities," and "information highways" that were found in the leading computer, electronics, and telecommunications magazines that Steve regularly read.

His interest piqued, Steve continued to read the Virtual Entrepreneur's message:

> I have also met a lot of low-tech virtual entrepreneurs! However, I have come to learn that even low-tech virtual entrepreneurs are usually more computer literate and savvy than most traditional managers. Computer literacy is essential for aspiring 21st century entrepreneurs!

Steve found himself nodding agreement with the Virtual Entrepreneur's assessment. He sensed that a higher degree of computer expertise was needed in order to become a virtual entrepreneur, and he knew that he had mastered that set of skills. In fact, he wondered how any contemporary theory of management could avoid taking computers and information technology into account.

Steve turned his attention back to the Virtual Entrepreneur's message:

> Let me give you a quick-and-dirty description of a virtual entrepreneur. A virtual entrepreneur is a visionary leader who is committed to starting a company that has a laser-tight business focus. This entrepreneur invests nearly all of his resources into his company's core competencies, and he outsources everything else to a network of world-class strategic partners.
>
> Moreover, a virtual entrepreneur seeks speed and flexibility in all of his company's day-to-day activities, and therefore relies heavily on the latest advances in information management and electronic commerce technology. I know that this is a screen full, yet these management concepts will become clearer with use.
>
> Please E-mail your fax number to me, and in return I will fax you some classic case studies from my electronic business library that further describe the essentials of virtual entrepreneurship. Happy Navigating - The Virtual Entrepreneur.

Steve Cole was curious about how the Virtual Entrepreneur had anticipated that he had a fax machine. In actuality, Steve's home office was highly automated, with a modem-equipped computer, color laser printer, plain paper facsimile machine, photocopier, cable television, and a state-of-the-art phone and answering machine.

Steve quickly E-mailed his fax number to the Virtual Entrepreneur and eagerly awaited a reply.

PROFILES OF "VIRTUALPRENEURS"

It was just after dinner when Steve heard his new plain paper fax machine activate and begin printing an incoming message.

He hurried over to his workstation and picked up the cover page of the incoming fax. He smiled for a couple of reasons. First, the enhanced resolution feature on his fax machine yielded a crystal-clear printout. And second, the incoming message was from the Virtual Entrepreneur.

Here are the classic case studies I promised you. I faxed three of my favorite cases to acquaint you with some of the more pioneering virtual entrepreneurs. I must point out that these summaries highlight only what I found interesting in the articles I reviewed. Therefore, I have provided the references in my summaries in case you want to get a copy of the original story.

If you are interested in learning more about virtual entrepreneurship once you read these cases, then let's get together soon and I'll show you around my own virtual company. Let me know your decision via E-mail, fax, or a cellular phone call. You already have my E-mail address. My fax and cellular phone numbers appear in the header of this message. Best Regards - The Virtual Entrepreneur.

The fax cover sheet informed Steve to expect nine pages, and nine pages was exactly what he received.

Steve walked into his modern kitchen, got some freshly brewed Kenyan coffee, and sat down at the kitchen table to read the three case studies. He took out a fluorescent yellow highlighter to isolate the key points.

FAX REPORT
The Pioneers of Virtual Entrepreneurship

Case Study 1:
Walden Paddlers, "The Ultimate Virtual Company"

Sources: *Inc. Magazine* and *Boston Magazine*

Edward Welles and Robert Crawford did an outstanding job of describing one of the first virtual companies in *Inc. Magazine* and *Boston Magazine*, respectively. Welles and Crawford described how Paul Farrow, a small business owner, launched Walden Paddlers, a virtual enterprise consisting of only one employee and a creative network of suppliers and retailers. These two business reporters described how Farrow, in just a ten-month period, used virtual management strategies to design, produce, and market a technically sophisticated kayak which was built from recycled plastic. Moreover, the environmentally friendly kayak was sold at a price that significantly undercut its competition, even though it was designed to out-maneuver much of the competition.

Some of the points that really impressed me about this pioneering virtual company are listed below.

Farrow's Concept of Virtual Management

I was intrigued with some key points that Farrow made about virtual management. A synopsis of his more noteworthy points follows:

■ A true "virtual corporation" outsources just about everything in pursuit of low overhead, speed to market, eternal flexibility, and leading-edge products, services, and technologies.

Virtual entrepreneurs must be able to keep tight control over their areas of expertise while subcontracting out everything else. Moreover, this article clearly points out that virtual companies are needed now more than ever, since companies in the 21st century must increasingly specialize in order to compete in more complex and competitive marketplaces.

■ Paul Farrow believes that most people work smarter, more productively, and cheaper when they work alone or in small groups. Hence, he never really considered staffing a full-blown manufacturing and marketing organization that would eventually prove slow to market, costly, and overly bureaucratic. By building a network-based virtual company instead of a multi-layered hierarchal corporation, Farrow knew he would create a whole that would be much greater than the sum of its parts.

■ Farrow seems to have rejected the trappings of the lavish corporate headquarters. Instead, his Zen-like workspace includes a work cubicle, an undersized metal desk, and a work bench with a sparse array of tools, clamps, and glues. An elaborate corporate office is not important to virtual entrepreneurs like Farrow, since their partners are decentralized throughout the network. However, in true virtual management form, Farrow does rely on a fax machine and a phone to provide him with 24 hour access to his network of partners.

A Guiding Vision

Farrow had a vision that he could expand the kayak market by designing a boat that even novices could easily maneuver. His research revealed that nearly all of the kayaks on the market were very "temperamental"—that is, they could easily tip over when someone stepped into them. Therefore, his network of partners had to be able to add some novel design features to ensure that Walden Paddler kayaks could be easily maneuvered by young and old novices alike, and not just by highly skilled kayakers. Farrow communicated this vision in a well-thought-out written plan.

Niche Focus

Farrow excelled at marketing research! He constantly met with boating organizations, read their literature, and talked to boat dealers. He then narrowed his focus to kayaks, a type of recreational boat which had tremendous potential for Farrow's virtual company. This laser-tight niche focus seems to be a universal skill of all virtual entrepreneurs.

While demarcating his niche, Farrow discovered that prices for traditional kayaks ranged from $400 to $2,500, and a customer had to pay at least $600 to be assured a minimal level of quality. Farrow was able to rely on his network of experts to design a high-quality, high-performance kayak at under $400.

Farrow's market research also revealed that growing numbers of people wanted to get out into nature while undertaking solitary pursuits. Kayaking could easily fill this need. Farrow's kayaks were also built from recycled plastic, thus allowing Walden Paddlers to benefit from yet another emerging marketing trend - environmentalism.

By keeping a niche focus (i.e., a low cost, user-friendly, and environmentally correct kayak), Farrow ensured his virtual company a fighting chance in the recreational boating market space.

Focus on Core Competencies

Farrow focused almost exclusively on his core competencies, which included strategic planning, guerilla marketing, and deal-making. He outsourced everything else to his partners. Each "world-class partner" was then responsible for ensuring both speed to completion and quality in all of their contributions to Farrow's virtual enterprise. Virtual entrepreneurs appear to differ from typical entrepreneurs since they do not try to become a jack-of-all-trades.

It must take an incredible amount of discipline for virtual entrepreneurs to stay focused on their core competencies at all times!

Weaving a Web of Partners

Paul Farrow relied on a web of strategic alliances to limit his company's payroll to one person - himself. He demonstrated how the ultimate virtual company could have just one employee. Not counting himself, Farrow relied on six critical alliances in his core network, including: (1) an accountant, (2) a banker, (3) a lawyer, (4) a product designer, (5) a plastics manufacturer, and (6) a packaging designer. This core network was expanded further to include distributors who specialized in sports and recreation markets. By limiting his virtual company to himself, and by designing, recruiting, and aligning a network of world-class partners and distributors, Farrow was able to spread his financial risks, keep his costs down, and quickly deliver a high-quality product.

Reduced Development Time

It took Paul Farrow's virtual company only ten months to bring a high-performance kayak from the design stage to the marketplace. By partnering with only the best, Farrow never got slowed down by having to hire, train, and monitor a group of professionals who would then be expected to design, develop, and market the first Walden Paddler kayak. Farrow set tough time lines for his partners and himself. And more importantly, everyone was able to consistently meet or exceed these goals.

Streamlined Sales and Distribution

Another of Farrow's core competencies was the ability to clearly describe his product to potential dealers, and then show them how it could fit into their product lines as a novel offering. Since he kept expenses under tight control with the low overhead that characterizes many virtual enterprises, Farrow was able to offer his distributors margins that were about 10% higher than his competitors. He also knew how to whet the dealers' appetites for his product by giving them a clearly drawn brochure and a simple sales pitch that they could use to describe his kayak to potential customers. Finally, Farrow provided interested dealers with a few no-cost demonstration boats for thirty days to prime the sales pump. Needless to say, sales immediately took off!

High-Tech/Low-Tech

This case study reveals how the first virtual companies could have both a high-tech and a low-tech emphasis. For example, Farrow's product designer relied on the latest in computer-aided design software when creating the blueprints for the first kayak. Farrow also relied on a manufacturer who had over twenty-five years of experience in molding plastics, and who had the technological expertise and equipment to build kayaks from recycled plastic. Those were some of the high-tech underpinnings of this virtual company.

Some of the low-tech strategies dealt with sales and distribution. For example, Farrow selected retailers who would physically display his kayak on their showroom wall or floor. His only promotional piece was the traditional paper brochure. It seems likely that in the future Farrow will utilize higher-tech sales strategies such as in-store promotional videotapes, computer-assisted multimedia sales presentations, and the ability to order kayaks online. Virtual entrepreneurs, I believe, will always try to incorporate more and more computer-based strategies into their operations to improve communications, ensure speed to market, and reduce costs.

I'm impressed, Steve Cole thought as he took a sip of coffee. The Virtual Entrepreneur's first case study had given him a nice feel for some of the more important elements of a virtual company. Things like finding a niche, focusing on core competencies, building a network of partners, and ensuring speed to market. *I must read on!*

Steve eagerly turned his attention to the next case study.

Case Study 2:
Calyx & Carolla, "A Company of Alliances"

Sources: *Inc. Magazine, Business Week* and *Business Horizons*

This pioneering virtual corporation was described as an award-winning entrepreneurial startup in a number of well-respected business publications. For example, *Inc. Magazine* reported how Ruth Owades founded and managed Calyx & Carolla, a virtual company that sells cut flowers and plants. Owades wanted to jump-start her new catalog business by partnering with highly reputable companies. Some of the more intriguing dimensions of her virtual company are listed below.

Process Reengineering

In the cut flowers business, it typically takes ten days to move flowers from the growers' fields to the customers. The flowers must be cut, transported to a wholesaler, shipped to a distributor, transported to a retailer, displayed and arranged for customers, and then shipped again to the customers. Wow! Ruth Owades envisioned a totally reengineered and simplified process in which flowers would be cut and arranged one day and reach the customer the very next. She is definitely a high-speed entrepreneur!

Ruth Owades was able to cut out three middlemen and four to six days from the process. Customers call Calyx headquarters and order their flowers from an attractive picture in the mail-order catalog. Calyx then electronically transmits the order to its online network of growers by computer link-ups. The growers have been trained to immediately arrange and ship the flowers the same day, and customers receive nicely displayed flowers the next day.

In brief, Owades used process reengineering and computer link-ups as the cornerstones of her pioneering virtual company. The Calyx process put customers more in command of their orders and ensured more vibrant and longer lasting flowers. Parenthetically, it is no surprise that Owades now has a virtual storefront on the World Wide Web!

Network of Partners

Owades built a virtual company that was almost completely dependent on strategic alliances. Her partners included more than twenty-five well-respected growers and a blue-chip shipper - Federal Express. Owades methodically utilized twenty-eight steps to ensure extremely successful alliances, including: (1) conducting background checks on prospective partners, (2) researching and meeting her potential partners' business needs, (3) properly negotiating "win-win" deals with potential partners, (4) soliciting suggestions from her partners (especially in their areas of expertise!), and (5) making sure she always had the time to properly maintain winning relationships with her partners.

Ruth Owades also noted that only one in three business alliances is truly successful. Therefore, a virtual entrepreneur like herself has to select and recruit partners wisely while doing everything in her power to make sure the relationships continue to work. As an aside, Owades is not afraid to quickly sever ties with any partner for poor performance reasons.

Capitalize on Technology

Technology forms the nervous system of this virtual company. Owades' strategy of electronically linking up a network of growers using a computer network and fax machines provided a definite competitive advantage. An 800 phone number and a highly skilled group of operators provide customers with immediate access to the order department. In addition, Owades selected a shipper that not only offered competitive prices, but also installed a computerized package tracking system at her office. Customized database management software was developed to facilitate and track mail order sales and marketing initiatives. Finally, Owades regularly keeps in touch with all of her partners by phone and fax machine.

Steve Cole could see similarities between Owades and Farrow, two highly successful virtual entrepreneurs. Like Farrow, Owades maintained a niche focus (i.e., offering freshly cut, nicely arranged flowers the next day). She also built a company around a network of carefully selected strategic partners, and she skillfully utilized technology for competitive advantage. Also, both of these pioneering virtual entrepreneurs capitalized on high-speed management.

Steve slapped his hands on his thighs and said aloud, "The Virtual Entrepreneur is making his point!" He reached for the final case study.

Case Study 3:
Weiss, Peck & Greer, "Plugged into Wall Street"

Source: *Forbes Magazine*

This simplistic yet intriguing case study shows why virtual entrepreneurs can even exist within larger companies. (However, I think it is more popular these days to refer to internal entrepreneurs as "intrapreneurs.") *Forbes* published a case study about a virtual intrapreneur named Liz Greetham who is a life sciences mutual fund manager for the New York City investment firm of Weiss, Peck & Greer Venture Partners. Greetham manages over $150 million of pharmaceutical, health care, and biotechnology stocks.

The catch: This pioneering virtual intrapreneur conducts all of her business from Bermuda, which is about 700 nautical miles from Wall Street. Some of the more impressive virtual management skills utilized by Liz Greetham are listed below.

An Online Network of Support

In large part, Liz Greetham has been able to manage her mutual fund from Bermuda because of her online network of alliances. She uses a stock quote computer to receive real-time quotes over the wires. She tele-manages an executive assistant and a research associate who work out of her Wall

Street office. Greetham has access to her trader over the phone, and she can always call CEOs who head up companies in which she is thinking of investing. She can also log into online business information services to study investment opportunities herself if she needs to. Greetham's online business network, which includes traders, stock quote analysts, industry researchers, her executive assistant, and CEOs of investment targets, successfully contributes to her top-performing mutual fund.

Staying Electronically Connected

Liz Greetham has skillfully integrated her computers, telephones, and other telecommunications equipment to guarantee her success as a telecommuting virtual manager. For example, her beachfront condominium office has five different phone lines: two voice, one fax, one modem line dedicated to the real-time quote service, and one modem line linked directly to her Wall Street office. Her investment research is readily accessible on both desktop and laptop portable computers.

Liz Greetham feels very comfortable working anywhere she can find a couple of phone jacks! High-tech virtual entrepreneurs really know how to set up shop on lucrative information networks and highways.

Focus on Core Competencies

The ultimate secret to Liz Greetham's success is that she skillfully focuses all of her resources on her core competency - selecting winning stocks for her life sciences fund. She requests, and then integrates, all incoming research and information for one purpose: to determine if she should buy, hold, or sell her life sciences stocks. She is not distracted by exhaustive business meetings, time-consuming travel, and office politics. Moreover, Greetham buffers herself against excessive job stress by avoiding the madness of Wall Street and by enjoying the tranquility of Bermuda, where she can swim and relax on the beaches.

Business is usually so much easier, enjoyable, and profitable for virtual entrepreneurs who do not try to overextend themselves to the breaking point.

I'm starting to see the connections, thought Steve. Like Farrow and Owades, Liz Greetham relied on a network of key resources. She was also very skilled at focusing on her core competencies at all times.

Steve saw that all three of the pioneering virtualpreneurs in the case studies shared several characteristics: (1) they had a laser-tight business focus, (2) they excelled in their core competencies, (3) they surrounded themselves with a successful network of strategic partners, and (4) they sought speed and flexibility in all of their day-to-day work activities.

After reviewing these case studies on virtual entrepreneurship, Steve knew exactly what he would do next. *I'm going to call the Virtual Entrepreneur tomorrow and see if he will teach me how to start my own successful virtual enterprise!*

FIVE GUIDING PRINCIPLES

At 10:00 the next morning, Steve Cole received an answering machine message that provided the Virtual Entrepreneur's 800 pager number, and he immediately called it. At the beep, Steve left his name and phone number and the following voice-mail message: "After reviewing your case studies of pioneering virtual entrepreneurs, I remain very interested in learning how to become a virtual entrepreneur. Please call me so we can set up a meeting as soon as possible." Steve was impressed that the Virtual Entrepreneur was so conveniently accessible through wireless paging technology.

Steve's phone rang at approximately 1:00 that afternoon. He eagerly answered after the first ring.

"Hello, Steve, this is the Virtual Entrepreneur. Sorry it took me so long to call you back, but I'm at the Pacific Golf Course driving range getting a lesson in short iron play. It's a good thing I brought my cellular phone! How can I be of assistance?"

Steve had been feeling a little apprehensive about talking to the Virtual Entrepreneur over the phone. After all, their first few communications had been through online chat rooms, E-mail, fax, and voice mail. But he was immediately reassured by the Virtual Entrepreneur's warm, confident tone.

"Thanks for calling me back so promptly," Steve said. "Could we get together sometime soon to discuss virtual management? We can discuss your consulting fee, too."

"No need to discuss fees!" the Virtual Entrepreneur said with a chuckle. "I'm in the sports and recreation business, not management consulting."

"But…if you aren't a consultant, why are you taking the time to introduce me to virtual entrepreneurship?"

"Steve, metaphysicists might say we are benefactors of 'synchronicity.' That is, for whatever reason and against all odds, we were both visiting the chat room at *The Entrepreneur's Network* Web site at the exact same date and time. We were also interested in the very same topic – contemporary management paradigms for entrepreneurs. I simply can't chalk up our first encounter to chance alone!"

Steve smiled. Maybe the Virtual Entrepreneur was right! "It's very generous of you to help me."

"I was also mentored by a virtual entrepreneur," the Virtual Entrepreneur continued. "I met her on the golf course, of all places. The lessons I learned from her helped me to launch a multi-million dollar virtual company called Night Vision Sports."

"Really?" Steve was excited to hear that the Virtual Entrepreneur had been so successful at incorporating what he had learned from his mentor. *Maybe I can do that, too!* Steve thought.

"I don't want to dwell on the details of my own education in virtual entrepreneurship, but I'm very sincere in my desire to pass on to you what I have learned from my mentor. This is one way I can contribute to an entrepreneurial revolution." The Virtual Entrepreneur paused, then added, "There's only one stipulation."

"What's that?" Steve felt sure that he would be willing to do whatever the Virtual Entrepreneur asked.

"You must promise to someday share this information, free of charge, with your own protégé. This is the same promise I was asked to make."

"Your offer sounds extremely generous, and I accept it!" Steve said eagerly. "I promise to freely pass on any knowledge that I gain from our meetings." Steve was pleased to make that promise.

He also felt sure that his relationship with the Virtual Entrepreneur would be built around a sense of trust and sharing.

———————————

The first face-to-face meeting between Steve Cole and the Virtual Entrepreneur was held at The Wharf, a rustic seafood restaurant overlooking a scenic oceanside golf course. They met at 1:00 in the afternoon.

"Hello, I'm Steve Cole. I'm very pleased to finally meet you in person." Steve extended his hand and was impressed with the strength of the Virtual Entrepreneur's handshake.

"Steve, I'm glad to meet you in person at last!" The Virtual Entrepreneur was tanned and fit-looking in casual slacks and a cotton knit shirt. He carried a slim leather attaché case. "I'm especially glad that our first meeting is at one of my favorite restaurants. Hopefully, we will also get to see some outstanding golf shots on the 18th hole that's nestled between this restaurant and the ocean. It's a long par five that sometimes requires a solid drive and two fairway wood shots from even the best of golfers." The Virtual Entrepreneur pointed through the restaurant's window to trace the long and winding par five for Steve.

The headwaiter seemed to know the Virtual Entrepreneur. Consequently, Steve and his soon-to-be mentor were given a prime table that overlooked the 18th hole. Before being seated, both Steve and the Virtual Entrepreneur stood at the window and admired the beauty of the oceanfront course.

When they finally sat down at the linen-draped table, the Virtual Entrepreneur placed his attaché case on the table in front of him and said, "I'm glad the three case studies I faxed you were sufficient to pique your interest in virtual entrepreneurship. They are three of the classic case studies in virtual management, but there were many others I thought about faxing, too." He smiled. "I decided I shouldn't give you information overload."

"I'd like to hear about any others that you think might be helpful," Steve said. "Can you think of any in particular?"

The Virtual Entrepreneur nodded. "Jeff and Mary Freeman come to mind. The Freemans founded Front Porch Computers, a four million dollar a year internationally focused small business. By spending less than $200 a month to post a classified ad on one of the nation's leading online services, the Freemans were able to inexpensively sell personal computers and other hardware to bargain-hunting customers in Europe, South America, and Asia. And their virtual company literally evolved from an online storefront that the Freemans ran from their house."

Steve tried to link the Freeman case study to the other three he had studied. Again, he saw some similarities, including a niche focus (using an online storefront to sell inexpensive computers to overseas clients), a reliance on technology for competitive advantage, and a small staff of full-time employees who networked with an online information service to gain immediate access, via an information highway, to millions of international customers.

"Are there other interesting cases that come to mind?" he asked.

"I looked at many," the Virtual Entrepreneur replied. "I studied and analyzed all available case studies in order to identify the common principles, management styles, and organizational designs that cut across the most successful virtual companies."

"Why did you go to so much trouble? Don't bookstores already carry texts on entrepreneurship that you could have studied?"

"Unfortunately, they don't! The standard books on how to become a successful entrepreneur focus primarily on the dominant personality traits of winning entrepreneurs, yet they fail to introduce aspiring entrepreneurs to contemporary models of organizational design and management. Personality traits such as self-confidence, optimism, persistence, calculated risk-taking, and need for achievement are usually examined in these traditional texts. In fact, I brought you a self-scoring questionnaire that will allow you to determine if you possess the more traditional entrepreneurial personality traits."

The Virtual Entrepreneur opened his attaché case and withdrew a sheet of paper which he handed to Steve. Steve saw that it was a twenty-item questionnaire. *(See Inset 1.)*

"While this questionnaire assesses important psychological traits for any business person to possess," said the Virtual Entrepreneur, "I was convinced that the number one reason that contemporary entrepreneurs succeed was not because of their personality alone, but because most winning entrepreneurs are able to quickly recognize, and then skillfully prosper from, unique business opportunities. I was determined to prove this point with my own company, Night Vision Sports!"

"That's exciting," Steve said. "What unique business opportunity did you recognize?"

The Virtual Entrepreneur smiled. "You'll know in due time. More importantly, you'll learn how to find your own unique opportunity and turn it into a profitable business."

"I can hardly wait!" Steve exclaimed. He looked down at the questionnaire. "I've personally heard many small business experts state that the entrepreneurial personality is the sole determinant of business success. I always thought that such a notion was a silly idea. In fact, some experts have gone so far as to suggest that the entrepreneurial personality is inborn! Your position, on the other hand, seems to be that the successful entrepreneur must be mentally and emotionally equipped to start and persistently manage a new business, yet must also be extremely skilled at quickly identifying and then exploiting new business opportunities."

The Virtual Entrepreneur smiled and nodded. "That's correct! I know many self-confident and ambitious entrepreneurs who have failed in business because they lacked a successful model of small business design and management. Using psychological personality traits alone to explain successful entrepreneurship is an oversimplified and misleading approach."

Steve listened intently as the Virtual Entrepreneur provided yet another important reason for his study.

"I have also been troubled by some statistics that reveal that anywhere from 60% to 90% of all entrepreneurial ventures eventually fail. I had to ask myself an important question: How good could the available theories on entrepreneurship be if there are so many small business casualties?"

Inset 1

"The Entrepreneurial Personality"
A Self-Test

Characteristic: (Circle your answers)	No	?	Yes
1. Are you an optimistic person?	0	1	2
2. Do you get easily frustrated and give up easily?	2	1	0
3. Are you competitive?	0	1	2
4. Do you prefer an easy-going lifestyle?	2	1	0
5. Are you able to establish and reach your own goals when working?	0	1	2
6. Do you gain more enjoyment from planning activities than from carrying them out?	2	1	0
7. Are you a good negotiator who is able to persuade others to accept your point of view?	0	1	2
8. Do you stick to a plan even when it is seriously failing?	2	1	0
9. Are you able to effectively cope with job stress and uncertainty?	0	1	2
10. Do you believe that being successful in business is largely a matter of hard work?	0	1	2
11. Are you a good problem solver?	0	1	2
12. Are you lacking in self-confidence?	2	1	0
13. Do others think you are ambitious and achievement oriented?	0	1	2
14. Do you take big risks in life without thinking through all of the consequences?	2	1	0
15. Are you comfortable being at the center of the action?	0	1	2
16. Do you have trouble managing your time?	2	1	0

	No	?	Yes
17. Do you possess the energy and endurance to start you own company?	0	1	2
18. Do you prefer to have enough extra time in the week for a full social life?	2	1	0
19. Are you able to say "no" to your friends and colleagues without feeling guilty?	0	1	2
20. Do you prefer to be your own boss?	0	1	2

Self-Scoring Instructions:

a) Make sure you answered all questions.

b) Add up your total points and record your answer here.

Total Score = _____

c) Determine your entrepreneurial profile below.

Scoring Range Interpretation:

34-40   Very strong entrepreneurial potential. Go for it!

26-33   Strong in many areas, yet opportunities for self-development still exist. Work on those items for which you did not receive any points.

18-25   Borderline potential. Review your answers to identify those areas of your entrepreneurial personality that need development.

10-17   Your potential is doubtful unless you undergo some serious attitude and behavior changes.

0-9   Entrepreneurship is probably not for you.

"You make a great point," Steve conceded. "Tell me more."

"I wanted to develop a more contemporary and effective model of entrepreneurial management that could serve as the foundation for my own virtual company," the Virtual Entrepreneur continued. "After studying the lessons shared by my mentor and a large number of virtual companies over a two-year period, I have identified five guiding principles of virtual management. In my opinion, they are the five most important factors that contribute to the success of most virtual companies. While there are surely other principles to consider, these five form the heart and soul of my virtual enterprise."

"So another major reason you conducted the study was to identify a new model of entrepreneurship that could serve as the blueprint for your own company," Steve reflected.

"Right! Hopefully, you'll be able to benefit from learning my five principles, too. I'll share a brief overview of my program with you after we eat." The Virtual Entrepreneur glanced at the waiter, who was approaching their table. "For now, let's order."

Steve and his mentor chatted amiably as they enjoyed some fresh chowder and a crab and avocado salad. Steve was pleased that he was already feeling so comfortable with the Virtual Entrepreneur.

When his second cup of Kona coffee was being served, the Virtual Entrepreneur looked across the table at Steve and said, "Ready for an overview of my program?"

"You bet!" Steve quickly pulled out his personal digital assistant so he would be ready to key in some notes. His heart rate picked up a little as a feeling of anticipation flooded through him.

The Virtual Entrepreneur began by handing Steve a single sheet of paper that summarized his five principles. Steve ran his eyes down over the sheet as he waited for the Virtual Entrepreneur's overview. *(See Inset 2.)*

"Steve, my first principle is to identify niche opportunities. Virtual entrepreneurs must be skilled at quickly recognizing and then exploiting new business opportunities before their competitors.

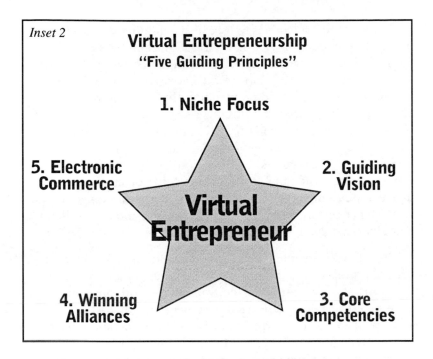

Inset 2

Virtual Entrepreneurship
"Five Guiding Principles"

1. Niche Focus

5. Electronic Commerce

2. Guiding Vision

Virtual Entrepreneur

4. Winning Alliances

3. Core Competencies

This skill will become even more important in the future as our markets become more competitive and congested. Paul Farrow was able to accomplish this by identifying and exploiting the very narrow market niche of low-cost, user-friendly, and environmentally correct kayaks. Ruth Owades of Calyx & Carolla capitalized on the opportunity to cleverly reengineer and speed up the process of bringing cut flowers to market. Both of these virtual entrepreneurs skillfully identified and then quickly seized new market niches."

Steve Cole nodded thoughtfully. He liked the concise way the Virtual Entrepreneur summarized his points. Again, he was curious about the niche opportunity that had launched the Virtual Entrepreneur's own company. *You'll know in due time,* the Virtual Entrepreneur had said. Steve decided to reign in his impatience and pay attention as the Virtual Entrepreneur presented the lessons at his own pace.

"My second principle is to establish a guiding vision," the Virtual Entrepreneur continued. "Virtual entrepreneurs are no different from any successful executive when it comes to the need to exhibit visionary leadership. Paul Farrow envisioned a way to market a low-cost, high-quality kayak that was ecologically safe. His vision also included bringing recreational kayaking to the masses. Therefore, all of his activities, ranging from selecting partners to manufacturing an environmentally correct kayak from recycled plastic, were guided by his vision. Ruth Owades also had a strong guiding vision that fresh flowers could be cut and arranged in one day by a network of growers so they could be express shipped to reach her customers by the next day. Her vision drove all of her reengineering and computerization initiatives.

"My third principle is to always focus on core competencies. Virtual entrepreneurs do not try to be a jack-of-all-trades! They focus instead on their core competencies and subcontract or outsource everything else. For instance, Farrow focused on his marketing and deal-making expertise, Owades capitalized on her process reengineering skills and knowledge of the cut flowers industry, and Liz Greetham of Weiss, Peck & Greer, focused her energies on making well-informed and profitable investment decisions."

The Virtual Entrepreneur paused to sip some Kona coffee. He was exuding an almost palpable aura of enthusiasm as he talked about his guiding principles of virtual entrepreneurship, and the excitement was running through Steve Cole's bloodstream, too.

"My fourth principle is probably the most important," the Virtual Entrepreneur went on after setting his cup on the table. "Virtual entrepreneurs must be able to intelligently establish winning alliances. Outsourcing works well only if world-class partners are properly selected, aligned, and integrated. For instance, Farrow developed his web of core partners along with an expanded network of distributors. Owades had a streamlined network of alliances that included dependable growers and a top-tier shipper. And Greetham's electronic network formed the nervous system of her virtual operation. Most importantly, these virtual entrepreneurs' partners and allies all felt a sense of co-destiny with the other members of their network."

"It must be challenging to pull together and coordinate a strong network of business experts," Steve observed.

"Yes it is! A critical aspect of developing winning alliances is to always nurture a high-trust culture. Virtualpreneurs like Paul Farrow and Ruth Owades always strive to cut win-win deals with their partners to ensure that all members of the alliance feel a sense of co-destiny. Also, successful virtualpreneurs must continuously integrate and coordinate all of their partners' activities to ensure that all members of the network stay on schedule and contribute their fair share. This type of skillful coordination builds trust and confidence, too. The higher the sense of trust between partners, the longer the success of the virtual enterprise will endure."

Steve could see why the Virtual Entrepreneur was so enthusiastic about the concepts. He felt sure that the specifics would be presented when he saw the Virtual Entrepreneur's own company.

The Virtual Entrepreneur took another sip of coffee before he continued. "As an aside, one feature of all virtual entrepreneurs' visions is to create a cost-efficient, network-based company with low overhead. Paul Farrow of Walden Paddlers controlled costs by working in a garage office that consisted of a cubicle, an under-sized desk, and a workbench. The Freemans launched an internationally focused computer company from their own rural home in the United States. Virtual entrepreneurs never envision the need for a large, centralized, and costly corporate office. In fact, they avoid building overly bureaucratic empires. Virtual entrepreneurs are more interested in selecting, aligning, and motivating a decentralized network of world-class partners who will share in the financial costs and risks of their virtual company."

Steve Cole keyed in some notes on his digital assistant. He was beginning to understand how business strategies that dealt with niche marketing, visionary leadership, core competencies, and winning alliances could form the foundation of a virtual enterprise. Yet he was eager to learn even more. "Do virtual entrepreneurs rely heavily on computer technology?"

The Virtual Entrepreneur nodded, a faint smile on his lips. "You anticipated my fifth and final principle. Virtual entrepreneurs always strive to master computers and related information technology. At the heart of almost every virtual entrepreneur's company is an innovative application of computer-based technology. Farrow relied on computer-aided product design technology. Owades selected a shipper who would install a computerized package tracking system in her office. Greetham was electronically linked to her stock quote service, brokers, researchers, and corporate headquarters. And the Freemans at Front Porch Computers utilized an online ordering system to access international customers who subscribed to a leading online service. Virtual entrepreneurs constantly search for new ways to benefit from the very latest advances in technology.

"The skillful application of technology also ensures speed to market. And virtual entrepreneurs are very proficient high-speed managers. They use technology to speed up and reengineer all critical cycle times at their companies, ranging from product development to high-speed selling. Remember, Farrow brought a highly innovative kayak from the design stage to the marketplace in only ten months through the use of computer-aided product design. Owades used technology to reduce the amount of time it took to get cut flowers from the growers' fields to the customers from ten days to two days. Greetham used technology to access real-time stock quote information so she could make split-second investment decisions. Virtualpreneurs are also increasingly using technology to make themselves more accessible to customers through electronic commerce on the Internet."

Steve nodded. "Virtual storefronts in cyberspace. I've surfed the Web. Some of those online stores are extremely well designed."

"You're right!" the Virtual Entrepreneur agreed. "And designing an effective Web site is something of an art in itself. We'll talk more about this cutting-edge concept later. The main point I wanted to make is that virtual entrepreneurs utilize technology to become outstanding time-based competitors."

Steve took a moment to think about everything the Virtual Entrepreneur had said. The Virtual Entrepreneur had just described a simplistic yet elegant model of contemporary entrepreneurship. The first three principles emphasized three important leadership skills routinely exhibited by highly talented entrepreneurs – providing focus, vision, and discipline, respectively.

The final two principles dealt with organizational design issues. Virtual entrepreneurs must be skilled at building networked companies that capitalize, at least in part, on contemporary technologies such as electronic commerce systems.

"That's an overview of my model, Steve," the Virtual Entrepreneur said, leaning back in his chair. "If you're still interested, I am now ready to introduce you to my own virtual company."

"Am I interested?" Steve exclaimed. "Are you kidding?"

The Virtual Entrepreneur smiled, obviously pleased with Steve's enthusiasm. "Let's meet at 9:00 tomorrow evening at the Pacific Golf Course and Resort over on Ocean Front Road. What do you say?"

"Let's do it!" Steve exclaimed. Then he paused as a thought struck him. "But why go to a golf course at that late hour?"

The Virtual Entrepreneur only laughed.

PRINCIPLE 1:
IDENTIFY NICHE OPPORTUNITIES

When Steve Cole pulled into the parking lot of the Pacific Golf Course and Resort at 8:55 p.m., the lot was nearly empty. The sky was dark in the east, but still streaked with deep orange and red and purple light in the west.

Steve had played this course a few times as a teenager. As he approached the driving range, he saw the Virtual Entrepreneur hitting slow, rising drives with a metal-headed driver. The drives were easily sailing past the 250 yard marker.

"Glad you could make it, Steve," the Virtual Entrepreneur said. "This is the perfect time and place for me to teach you about the first principle of virtualpreneuring – identifying niche opportunities."

"I'm glad you invited me," Steve said, looking out over the fairway. Deep shadows were gathering in the hollows. "It's too bad we couldn't meet earlier in the day so we could play a round of golf."

The Virtual Entrepreneur didn't reply directly to Steve's comment. Instead, he said, "Golf has been around for a long time, but its popularity has really been surging in the past few years. Golf had become a multi-billion dollar industry by the early 1990's. In fact, there were over twenty-four million golfers in the United States alone during that time, and estimates are that the number of golfers will probably double by the end of the century."

"Sounds as if you've done some research," Steve observed.

"I conducted a quick-and-dirty marketing study on the Internet. I also found out that the growth in expected demand will exceed the development rate of new golf courses. That means there will be more crowding on the courses and more frustrated golfers." The Virtual Entrepreneur paused, then gestured toward a bench near the first tee. "Let's have a seat."

Steve followed the Virtual Entrepreneur to the bench. It was starting to acquire a thin layer of nighttime dew, so the Virtual Entrepreneur wiped it off with his golf towel.

"We'll sit at the exact spot where, a few years ago, I had my first 'eureka' that led to Night Vision Sports. I was sitting on this very bench at dusk when I realized that a lucrative market niche was staring me right in the face." The Virtual Entrepreneur smiled as he began to reminisce, but his facial expression transformed to that of a hawk as he scanned the darkening horizon that framed the golf course.

Steve felt a renewed thrill of anticipation surge through him. "What was it like? That moment of insight, I mean."

"Exhilarating," the Virtual Entrepreneur answered simply.

"So what was it?" Steve pressed when the Virtual Entrepreneur paused. "What was the lucrative market niche you discovered?"

Instead of answering his question directly, the Virtual Entrepreneur said, "Steve, tell me what you see as you look out over the golf course, the adjoining putting green, and the driving range. Tell me about the first impression that comes to your mind."

Steve surveyed the entire area in front of him. "Well…it's getting pretty dark, but I can see some golfers walking swiftly up the 18th fairway. They're probably trying to finish their round before it gets too dark. There's another foursome one hole back." He shook his head in sympathy. "They'll never finish their round!" He strained his eyes through the gathering darkness. "I don't see any other golfers."

"You've got good night vision!" the Virtual Entrepreneur praised. "There's hardly anyone on the course, even though this is a very enjoyable and challenging game that people love to play. A lot of people would play golf at night if they could see well enough. While conducting some research on the Internet, I learned that in Alaska, highly skilled golf pros and amateurs often work on their games around the clock during the summer when the sun never sets. For those of us who don't live in Alaska, the night's darkness is like a steel gate that keeps golfers away from this playground until the crack of dawn."

"But most golfers have to work during the day," Steve pointed out. "So they never have enough time to play their favorite sport."

The first foursome had reached the 18th green. All four golfers had apparently hit bad approach shots, and they were repeatedly missing their putts. Steve knew they were rushing their shots in order to complete their round of golf before total darkness set in. Their haste was obviously leading to high scores and frustration on the final hole.

"Steve, as simple as this may sound, you have successfully de-scribed the major element of my golden niche opportunity," the Virtual Entrepreneur said. "My 'eureka' was that golfers, espe-cially the more obsessive kind, would be willing to pay a pretty penny for something that would let them play golf at night. Don't you agree?"

Steve turned to face the Virtual Entrepreneur. "Sure!"

"Therefore, my ultimate goal was to develop a strategy whereby I could peel back the night for golfers so they could play golf in the dark." The Virtual Entrepreneur smiled. "Actually, I had prob-ably been subconsciously aware of this unique niche opportunity for a year or more before I decided to start Night Vision Sports. I often found myself ruminating about factors that suggest how popu-lar nighttime golf could be. Namely, the recent invention and popu-larity of golf balls that glow in the dark, the historic availability and success of lighted driving ranges, and the development of a few lighted par-3 executive golf courses that are prohibitively ex-pensive to develop and operate."

Steve nodded. "You're right. Golf enthusiasts are willing to go to great lengths to enjoy their sport at any time, day or night."

"Then there are those indoor virtual reality-based golf centers that simulate a game of golf," the Virtual Entrepreneur went on. "Golfers simply hit their balls into a computerized screen that resembles a famous golf hole, and a computer readout lets them know how far and straight their shots were hit. Some of these simulations even include a nearby putting surface so that golfers can play a complete hole! And of course there are an abundance of video golf games on the market that allow golfers to at least *think* about golf strategy and club selection whenever they want."

Steve was impressed by the Virtual Entrepreneur's familiarity with the competitive product offerings. "I've tried the virtual reality golf centers," he said. "They're okay, but not the real thing."

"Right! The innovators who developed virtual reality centers were trying to create substitute environments whereby golfers could play golf around the clock. This was important to know, since these pioneers had already begun to develop my market.

"Yet I knew in my heart that glow balls, lighted courses, indoor simulations, and video games could not face the ultimate challenge of allowing die-hard golfers to play regulation golf courses at night, without lights, while still being able to observe and experience the course's aesthetic surroundings. That was my niche opportunity— the golf-at-night market for dedicated golfers!"

"That would certainly appeal to a lot of golfers!" Steve acknowledged.

"Of course, I couldn't base my entire plan on guesswork. I decided to conduct some market research to give me an estimate of how many golfers would be interested in playing golf at night. I didn't want to lose momentum by conducting a full-blown market research study, but I did want to identify the parameters of this potentially lucrative nighttime market. So I took the most direct route I could think of – I went to several representative golf courses so I could see how many twilight golfers were out there."

"I like the direct approach," Steve said. "But what, exactly, do you mean by 'twilight golfers?'"

"Twilight golfers usually play after work. They tee off with only enough time to play nine to twelve holes, if they're lucky. They're always frustrated by the fact that they don't have enough daylight hours left to finish a complete round before the sun sets. Most twilight golfers are lucky if they get to play for one to two hours before total darkness sets in, while a typical eighteen-hole round of daytime golf takes four to five hours."

"I see the opportunity!" Steve was impressed with how quickly yet thoroughly the Virtual Entrepreneur had explored his market niche. "What else did your market research reveal?"

"I found that nearly 15% of all golfers fall into the 'frustrated twilight golfer' category. That means that by the turn of the century, approximately 7.2 million golfers in the United States alone might be interested in nighttime golf. And this conservative estimate doesn't even take into account those people who want to play golf but don't have enough time for even twilight golf. Nor does it take into account the more fanatical golfers who always want to play at *any* time during the day or night. In addition, there are probably many heat-sensitive golfers who would rather play in the cool of the night. Needless to say, these promising figures motivated me to proceed with my entrepreneurial dream by founding Night Vision Sports."

Steve could see that the Virtual Entrepreneur had identified a unique, yet barely tapped, market niche. But Steve still had no idea how the Virtual Entrepreneur was able to service this niche.

As he was thinking about this, Steve caught a glimpse of the final foursome on the course. He had predicted that this group would never finish their round, but to his surprise, they were leisurely working their way up the 18th fairway. It was almost totally dark, and Steve could only see the golfers' silhouettes with the help of the moonlight.

Yet for some reason, this group did not seem to be rushing their shots as the previous group had done. And at least three of the golfers' fairway shots sounded as if they landed safely on or very near the green. Two of the golfers even shouted hello to the Virtual Entrepreneur.

How can they see us sitting here? Steve wondered. *How can they recognize the Virtual Entrepreneur in this darkness?*

"The members of that final foursome are friends of mine, Steve," the Virtual Entrepreneur said. "They were also my very first customers. They were the first golfers to test my unique approach to extending golfing hours into the nighttime. I'll be forever grateful for their support of Night Vision Sports."

The Virtual Entrepreneur was beaming with pride. He stood up and shook all of the golfers' hands as they headed off the green. Steve chose to stay near the bench and observe the scene. He was startled to see that each of the golfers was wearing a set of sleekly designed silver goggles that looked like virtual reality goggles without the computer hook-up. Although it was too dark to get a good look at the goggles, Steve did wonder if they were part of the Virtual Entrepreneur's secret.

They all walked together to the clubhouse, where the Virtual Entrepreneur chatted with his friends. Steve decided to review what he had learned from his first lesson. He pulled out his personal digital assistant, sat down at a lighted patio table near the clubhouse, and typed in some of the key points he had learned during the last forty-five minutes.

Principle #1: Identify Niche Opportunities

1. Skillfully anticipate future opportunities.

The Virtual Entrepreneur demonstrated excellent future vision. He knew that there would be a greater demand for access to high-quality regulation golf courses in the 21st century, yet the pace of developing these courses wouldn't keep up with demand. Therefore, the Virtual Entrepreneur planned to significantly extend the playing time of established regulation golf courses in order to absorb some of the increased demand.

2. Quickly access marketing information.

The Virtual Entrepreneur did his marketing homework using his online information service. He conducted some quick-and-dirty, yet very useful, market research studies to identify the projected number of golfers in general. He then conservatively forecasted the number of possible nighttime golfers. The Virtual Entrepreneur also identified various subgroups of golfers who might be most amenable to nighttime golf, including frustrated twilight golfers, people who wanted to play golf but didn't have the time for either daytime or twilight golf, heat-sensitive golfers, and golf fanatics who would play almost anywhere at any time. Even highly skilled golfers who wanted some extra practice would be receptive to nighttime golf!

3. Dominate unique market niches by maintaining a narrow focus.

The Virtual Entrepreneur focused on a narrow and unique subniche of the golf market. Instead of including daytime or even twilight golfing hours, he focused exclusively on nighttime golf. He was committed to further developing this newer segment of the market.

4. Clearly differentiate yourself from your competitors.

The Virtual Entrepreneur planned to accomplish this step in a number of ways. First, his focus on nighttime golf was a clear differentiating factor. Second, he was positioning himself to provide a service that was clearly different from glowing golf balls, lighted courses, indoor golf course simulations, and video games, to name a few. In addition, he was focusing on nighttime golf at regulation courses as opposed to lighted par-3 executive courses and driving ranges. This was targeted marketing at its best!

Steve Cole saved his input to a file, turned off his digital assistant, and put it in his pocket. The Virtual Entrepreneur's niche was looking more and more intriguing.

He looked up and realized that the Virtual Entrepreneur's friends had gone, and the Virtual Entrepreneur had been waiting patiently for him to finish his note-taking.

"Let's drive down the street and have some coffee," the Virtual Entrepreneur suggested. "I know it's late, but I want to describe my second principle to you as soon as possible. I want to take you through the exact steps I followed in founding my virtual enterprise."

Steve was all for that! The Virtual Entrepreneur was on a roll, and Steve was eager to absorb as much information as he could.

PRINCIPLE 2:
ESTABLISH A GUIDING VISION

The Virtual Entrepreneur invited Steve Cole to accompany him to an all-night bookstore that served flavored coffees. The bookstore was only a few minutes from a number of famous golf courses nestled between the Pacific Ocean and the Northern California mountain ranges.

Steve smelled freshly brewed vanilla coffee when they entered the store, and they sat at a table that was situated in the middle of some handmade bookshelves.

"Steve, I thought this would be a good time to discuss my second principle: establishing a guiding vision," the Virtual Entrepreneur said after they had ordered coffee. "I hope you don't mind the late hours."

"Not at all. I'm glad we're making such good progress." Steve was beginning to realize that the Virtual Entrepreneur truly loved the nighttime hours.

"Good! This principle follows closely on the heels of the first. Once the aspiring virtual entrepreneur has identified his niche opportunity, the next challenge is to develop a winning vision for turning that opportunity into a successful virtual company. I discovered through my studies that the most successful virtual entrepreneurs are visionary leaders. That is, they are highly skilled at creating winning visions of the future and applying these visions to jump-start their companies."

"What do you mean by a winning vision?" Steve asked.

"To me, a winning vision reflects the uniqueness of the company so that it clearly stands out from the competition. A winning vision also clarifies the company's purpose and direction, and therefore can be used to guide all of the company's strategies and actions. In a nutshell, it must inform and inspire."

Steve nodded thoughtfully. It seemed logical that all successful companies, including virtual enterprises, would require a guiding vision.

"A winning vision does even more for the leader of a virtual enterprise," the Virtual Entrepreneur continued after a sip of his café mocha. "It is the major strategy for signing up strategic partners to form a virtual corporation. It helps to join all of them around a common purpose. And if it's truly inspiring, strategic members of a unified virtual corporation become highly motivated to quickly transform the leader's vision into reality. Remember, a vision is only one person's dream of the future. It only becomes a *successful* vision if the dream is realized."

"Do you have any favorite corporate visions that you've studied over the years?" Steve asked.

"Interesting question. In fact, several memorable visions come to mind. A classic vision is Henry Ford's dream of widely affordable cars for average citizens. Steve Jobs, co-founder of Apple Computer, had a vision of a desktop computer for personal use in every household. Vice President Al Gore and others offered a seductive vision of a global information superhighway. There are many, many more."

"Excellent examples!" Steve acknowledged. "Those are definitely inspiring visions."

"But remember, Steve, visionary leaders are results-oriented people. Their visions must be realistic, desirable, and achievable. Most visionary leaders are pioneers who are venturing into unexplored territory. Yet these leaders know how to get their organizations moving toward new and oftentimes unfamiliar destinations." The Virtual Entrepreneur leaned back and finished off his café mocha.

Steve was eager to learn about the Virtual Entrepreneur's own vision. But he took a moment to savor the last of his coffee. It had a soothing taste, in addition to the much-needed late night caffeine pick-me-up.

As Steve's eyes casually scanned the bookstore, he remembered his own search through the management sections of bookstores. Few of the books he found were as interesting as the Virtual Entrepreneur's stories and lessons.

"What about your virtual company's vision?" he asked at last, putting down his empty cup. "Does it meet all the requirements of a winning vision?"

"I think it does, Steve. In fact, I've brought a copy of my vision for your review. I'll elaborate on its key points after you've read it." The Virtual Entrepreneur retrieved a single sheet of paper from his attaché case and handed it to Steve.

Steve opened the paper and read the clear, concise statement:

Night Vision Sports

This virtual enterprise is committed to offering the most innovative and stylish night vision glasses that allow golfers to play their beloved game at night on regulation golf courses.

"This vision includes a number of special properties," the Virtual Entrepreneur said after Steve had read the vision statement. "First, it clarifies both the purpose and the direction of Night Vision Sports. In brief, I want my company to offer stylish yet technologically sophisticated night vision glasses so golfers can play their favorite game at night on regulation courses. Period! As we discussed earlier, many golfers would love to be able to play this sacred game well into the night. And for too long, night vision goggles and scopes, which you will learn more about soon, have been unnecessarily restricted to military and police use."

Steve was all ears. This was the first time he had heard the Virtual Entrepreneur mention night vision glasses. Steve had actually become acquainted with night vision goggles in some popular movies he had recently watched. "I'm eager to hear about the special properties of your strategic vision."

"I also wanted my vision to reflect Night Vision Sports' unique organizational design," the Virtual Entrepreneur went on. "For instance, I wanted to develop a virtual corporation around a network of high-caliber strategic partners. These partners would provide the expertise my company needed in terms of research, product development, sales, and service. This type of networked organization would allow me to speed up product development, reach targeted customers more quickly, and most importantly, spread my costs and risks."

"And you actually made reference to a virtual organization in your vision," Steve said, nodding. "What other special properties does your vision possess?"

"I believe that a vision should always set standards of excellence and reflect high ideals. For example, I will always require that my night vision systems display the most innovative and stylish features on the market, and I emphasized *style* in my vision. My designers succeeded in making some creative and challenging design modifications to the traditional night vision scopes used by the military and police. That is, we succeeded in manufacturing ultra-light night vision glasses that golfers could comfortably wear when they played. Yet I must always make sure that my partners are keeping up a torrid pace of constant innovation."

"So I assume your version of night vision goggles are sleek, stylish, and lightweight."

"Exactly!" The Virtual Entrepreneur smiled. "I also wanted

my vision to be attainable. I knew that night vision technology already existed, so I would be merely upgrading and reapplying readily available technology as opposed to inventing brand new technology, which can be very time consuming and extremely risky. I also knew that there were some small high-tech companies that were struggling to make a transition from a shrinking military market to a potentially lucrative commercial market. And some of these high-tech companies produced night vision goggles."

"So you were prepared to immediately capitalize on some of the cut-backs in the military expenditures."

"Right! If my vision could inspire enthusiasm and encourage commitment from a talented company that already produced night vision goggles, I felt I would gain a head start in turning my dream into a reality."

Steve was impressed. He could see how important it was to have a strong yet succinct guiding vision. "I can't believe all of the important themes you've covered with such a clear, concise vision statement."

"There's still one more," said the Virtual Entrepreneur. I wanted to develop a vision that could be easily communicated and understood. A vision has to serve as a guide to strategy development and planning. Therefore, it has to reflect a clear-cut future goal so my strategic partners and I could develop the most relevant action steps for reaching the goal."

"And your ultimate goal is to always provide the most innovative and stylish night vision glasses to golfers so they can play well into the night," Steve said, summarizing the essence of the Virtual Entrepreneur's vision statement.

"Definitely!" the Virtual Entrepreneur confirmed. "And since my vision is pretty straightforward and targets golfers directly, I am able to easily communicate this message to the proper parties who have some degree of interest in this wonderful sport. This includes potential partners, investors, and customers, to name a few."

"But what if other sports enthusiasts get interested in this product? What then?" Steve wondered if the Virtual Entrepreneur's vision was too limiting.

"I felt it was critical that I first communicated a laser-focused vision that addressed a distinct market niche. My vision would then provide a clear-cut direction for all of my resource allocations and network building efforts. If new and potentially lucrative markets emerge, I'll update and revise my company's vision at that time. For instance, I think that both joggers and cyclists will someday gravitate toward night vision glasses, and a revised vision must accommodate these new customers. In this day and age, a strategic vision might only last anywhere from two to five years." The Virtual Entrepreneur pushed back his chair and got to his feet. "If you don't mind, I'd like to take a look at the latest books on golf and business. That's one reason I wanted to come here."

"Sure," Steve said. "You've given me a lot to think about!"

As the Virtual Entrepreneur disappeared around a large, freestanding bookcase, Steve leaned back in his chair and considered what he'd learned. He was awed by the Virtual Entrepreneur's use of vision as a virtual leadership strategy. It was easy to see why virtual entrepreneurs had to be visionary leaders. Steve was also eager to learn more about night vision glasses.

He got out his digital assistant and began recording his thoughts.

Principle #2: Establish a Guiding Vision

5. Create a believable vision of the future.

The Virtual Entrepreneur created an attractive, worthwhile, and achievable vision that clarified the purpose, direction, and uniqueness of his virtual enterprise. His vision is based on reasonable assumptions about the future of golf; that is, a select group of golfers would give anything to be able to play golf at night on a regulation course. In addition, golf course managers would probably be willing to extend their courses' playing hours to accommodate the growing demand. Night vision glasses for golf could help this situation. Finally, since the Virtual Entrepreneur's vision is tightly focused on nighttime golf, it comes across as being both unique and achievable.

6. Communicate your vision to persuade potential partners to commit their resources to achieving your dream.

This is one of the Virtual Entrepreneur's major strengths. His vision can be used to successfully recruit and join all of his partners together for a common purpose - to allow golfers the opportunity to play nighttime golf with the aid of stylish night vision glasses. In fact, I'll bet the Virtual Entrepreneur always tries to communicate his vision to potential investors and partners while they are overlooking a golf course at sunset. This strategy would enhance the impact of his message.

7. The vision must be transformed into reality.

The Virtual Entrepreneur's vision can be used to attract the commitment of his strategic partners. It can also be used to unify, focus, and motivate members of the network to develop high-quality, innovative, and stylish products in record time. Most importantly, all of the Virtual Entrepreneur's plans and activities are geared toward transforming his vision into reality.

8. The vision must be updated, expanded, or even narrowed when necessary.

A vision is a mental model of the future. And since the future can play itself out in different ways, the visionary leader must be willing to adapt his vision. For example, the Virtual Entrepreneur indicated that joggers and bikers might take a liking to his night vision glasses. Therefore, someday he must be willing to update and expand his vision to accommodate these new customers.

Steve saved the notes he'd made to himself, then turned off the digital assistant and put it away.

He was more excited than ever about the valuable lessons he was learning. The Virtual Entrepreneur had showed him first-hand how he'd applied the first two principles to Night Vision Sports by identifying a niche opportunity, and then by developing a clear, effective vision statement around which his company would be built.

Steve was eager to apply these principles to a business of his own, but he also felt a little anxiety. The Virtual Entrepreneur had certainly identified a niche opportunity with his night vision glasses for golfers. But what if Steve was unable to identify a niche opportunity? If he faltered with that first step, he would never have his own successful virtual company.

You aren't ready to cross that bridge yet, he chided himself. First he had to learn everything he could from the Virtual Entrepreneur.

Steve could hardly wait for the lessons to continue.

PRINCIPLE 3:
FOCUS ON CORE COMPETENCIES

The Virtual Entrepreneur was scheduled to meet Steve Cole at the Mountain Creek Golf Course at 9:30 in the evening. This was a beautiful course nestled between mountain creeks and pine trees. The main goal of the meeting was to discuss the third principle of the Virtual Entrepreneur's model. However, a secondary purpose was to introduce Steve Cole to Night Vision Sports' flagship product.

They met near the golf pro shop as planned.

"Hello, Steve," said the Virtual Entrepreneur. "I see you're properly dressed for a leisurely stroll on the golf course."

"I sure am," Steve said with a chuckle. He was wearing all-weather golf pants and a red Arnold Palmer sweater. "I imagine it can get rather damp and chilly on this course at night."

"The cooler temperature is invigorating! By the way, I brought something for you to try out during our stroll." The Virtual Entrepreneur handed Steve a sleek, silver-tone case the size of a four-by-ten-inch jewelry box.

Steve placed the case on a nearby table and noticed the Night Vision Sports label inscribed in smoky black letters across the top of the case. He carefully opened the box and found a sleek, stylish pair of night vision glasses sitting in the black velvet molding.

"They're beautiful!" he exclaimed. "Should I dare put them on?"

"In a moment," said the Virtual Entrepreneur, a half-smile of amusement playing on his lips. "First let me acquaint you with our top selling product—the Night Hawk 2000s. These glasses retail in the more exclusive golf shops for about $2,995. They were introduced just over a year ago, and we've already sold over 2,000 pairs, primarily to members of the more prestigious country clubs."

"The perfect gift for the golfer who has everything," Steve said with a laugh. He could hardly wait to try out the Night Hawks. Darkness had fallen completely by now. A few moon-silvered clouds appeared phosphorescent against the velvety blackness of the night sky. Faint moonlight dappled the area around them, outlining the shadowy shapes of nearby trees and shrubs.

"Owning a pair of Night Hawks has become a status symbol," said the Virtual Entrepreneur. "A *useful* status symbol, of course, and golfers are snapping them up to the tune of nearly $6 million a year in sales. Our revenues within this market niche are expected to grow at a rate of 50% or more per year while still yielding attractive profit margins."

"Impressive!" Steve said, still looking down at the night vision glasses.

"I want to explain why the success of this product is based on one of my own core competencies," the Virtual Entrepreneur said. "But first put on your Night Hawks so we can augment your night vision."

The Virtual Entrepreneur lifted the glasses out of the case and adjusted the strap so they snugly fit Steve's head. They were ultralight, weighing about three-quarters of a pound. Once they were properly adjusted, the Virtual Entrepreneur turned them on.

"Power is provided by two rechargeable triple-A batteries," he explained to Steve. "A computer chip controls the light detection and augmentation sensors."

"Holy cow!" Steve exclaimed with almost child-like wonder. "I can see the entire golf course as if it were daytime. This is fantastic!"

"Thanks, Steve. I'll bet your view looks something like the

electrified greenish daytime sky one sees right before a thunder-storm."

"I guess you're right," Steve said, turning his head this way and that. "But my night vision is definitely good enough for playing a round of golf. How do these goggles work?"

"Without getting into the sophisticated electronics and phys-ics, let me just say that my team has designed these glasses to maxi-mally amplify any available light from the setting sun, the stars, and the moon. In fact, we're able to increase available night light by 60,000 times. This process of increasing a person's ability to see under low-light conditions is called 'image intensification.' It was first used in the Vietnam War. Of course, the technology has improved greatly since then."

"You've certainly put the technology to good use," Steve said appreciatively, still looking around at the surroundings.

"One of my core competencies is to identify novel applications for existing technology, and that is exactly what I did in this case. Optical engineers who are affiliated with my virtual corporation designed our Night Hawks to be much more sophisticated in their capabilities than the cruder night vision goggles and monocular scopes used by the military and police. With our system, golfers can clearly see their drives land up to 300 yards away. Our sys-tems are also much lighter than traditional night vision scopes. And we have special features that allow golfers to fine-tune the focus, brightness, and field of vision to meet their preferences."

"Wow!" Steve said. "Can they tell you which iron to hit into a green?"

The Virtual Entrepreneur laughed. "I'm afraid not. Let's go out on the course so you can experience first-hand the freedom of seeing in the dark. I'll also explain my third principle – focusing on one's core competencies."

The Virtual Entrepreneur slipped on his own Night Hawks, and he and Steve changed into their golf spikes. They proceeded to stroll briskly down the 18th fairway.

Steve found himself in the midst of a wide variety of exciting night visions. The golf course fairways had a beautiful and almost surreal look of emerald green grass and yellowish sand traps. The surrounding trees appeared majestic, and Steve saw night owls and raccoons on their branches. The dew that covered the leaves looked like glistening jewels. The golf course had been transformed into nothing less than an enchanted forest.

"With my Night Hawks, night vision golfers can play their beloved sport and enjoy the breathtaking beauty of the night," the Virtual Entrepreneur said with unconcealed pride. "We are not only expanding the amount of time that golfers can play during a twenty-four-hour period, but we are also providing golfers access to a new world of beauty and tranquility."

That was, Steve had to admit, an unexpected side-benefit of the Night Hawks. The surroundings were beautiful with the amplified light, and the golf course at night was very peaceful.

After walking the length of the 18th hole, the Virtual Entrepreneur began to discuss the importance of focusing exclusively on one's core competencies.

"One of the most important aspects of a virtual corporation is to have each and every strategic partner focus on his or her core competencies." The Virtual Entrepreneur paused. "Before I go into that, I want to back up and encourage you to start only one business. The most successful entrepreneurs typically try to do only one thing, but they do that one thing very, very well."

"That makes sense," Steve said. "By concentrating on only one business, the entrepreneur will avoid losing focus and spreading his resources too thin."

"Exactly!" the Virtual Entrepreneur said, obviously pleased with Steve's quick perception. "For example, a boat designer who plans to design, construct, and then market his boats is actually trying to start three separate businesses. This is usually an impossible task and spells ultimate doom for many beginning entrepreneurs."

"So the virtual entrepreneur should contribute only his or her unique core competencies to the venture, and nothing more," Steve said. Then he realized that another lesson he'd learned earlier could be applied here, too. "That's where the strategic partners come in."

"Right again! Instead of doing everything himself, a virtual entrepreneur should do only what he does best, and he should design a network of strategic partners who are in separate businesses that complement the virtualpreneur's own core business. All of these discrete yet complementary companies can then become integrated under the virtual corporation's umbrella. For instance, a business writer could link up with a printer, a promoter, and book retailers."

"So each strategic partner must remain tightly focused on his own core business. And this discipline alone helps to ensure that all partners will become masters of their trade." Steve felt that he had accurately summarized, and then extended, the essence of the Virtual Entrepreneur's message.

The Virtual Entrepreneur smiled. "You're catching on very quickly, Steve! Not only should a company be in only one business at a time, but it should also dedicate nearly all of its resources to what it does best – its core competencies. Everything else should be outsourced. The companies that focus exclusively on their core competencies are the big winners in today's marketplace. I can think of several examples you'll recognize. Microsoft focuses exclusively on the timely development of high-quality and cutting-edge operating system software for personal computers. Honda maintains its core competencies in the design and manufacturing of engines and power trains of all sizes. And Sony's competencies are in the miniaturization of high-demand consumer electronics." The Virtual Entrepreneur paused to draw in a breath of cool night air and exhaled slowly. "It's beautiful out tonight."

"It sure is." Steve was appreciating the beauty of the night as seen through the Night Hawks, but his mind was tuned to the point that the Virtual Entrepreneur had made so well. Steve could see the importance of focusing on one's core competencies. This strategy, if adhered to by all members of the virtual corporation, would ensure a network of focused partners who would bring only their strengths to the coalition. "How did you identify your own core competencies?"

"I decided to approach it in a logical way," said the Virtual Entrepreneur. "First, I made a list of what I thought were my ten key entrepreneurial strengths, regardless of how silly they seemed. Later, I would boil that down to a few of my strongest core competencies. My ten key strengths, in no order of importance, were: 1) bottom-up marketing strategies, 2) strategic planning, 3) public relations and promotion, 4) deal-making and negotiations, 5) personal computer skills, 6) network and alliance building, 7) budgeting and finance, 8) motivating people, 9) creativity and innovation, and 10) understanding customers' preferences. From that, I had to boil it down to only two or three core competencies."

"How did you do that?"

"For a strength to be considered a core competency, it must pass three tests. First, it should be so strong that it can provide an entrepreneur with access to a wide variety of potentially lucrative markets. Second, it should make a significant and obvious contribution to the customer's perception of a high-quality end product. And finally, a core competency should be difficult for competitors to imitate."

Steve thought he knew how those criteria were used. "So those are the tests you used to narrow down the list of strengths to a few core competencies?"

"Exactly! I used a ten-point rating scale to rank my list of general strengths. But I realized that I could hardly be considered objective, so I asked a well-respected business associate to rank my strengths. He was very knowledgeable about my entrepreneurial skills and abilities, so I knew he could give me a fair ranking. The higher the ranking, the greater the probability that a skill was a core competency.

"I averaged these two separate rankings for each strength on my list and discovered that my core competencies included my ability to create new and novel markets through bottom-up marketing, my networking and alliance building skills, and my thorough knowledge of customers' preferences." He reached into his pocket for a folded sheet of paper, which he gave to Steve. "I brought a copy of my analysis sheet so you could review this methodology for determining core competencies."

Steve unfolded the worksheet and examined it before commenting. "So these three core competencies passed your three selection criteria." *(See inset 3.)*

"Right. My bottom-up marketing skills would help me to create and develop the novel night vision golf market. I also knew how to quickly pull together a group of strategic partners while negotiating some win-win terms. This second core competency is critical to starting and leading a virtual company. Finally, I really knew the preferences of my potential customers, the twilight golfers. By focusing almost exclusively on these three core competencies, it became clear that I should represent the marketing and business development arms of my virtual enterprise."

"And you relied on your partners to fill in the rest of the company's needs with their own core competencies."

The Virtual Entrepreneur nodded. "Right again. Of course, finding the right partners was another challenge. But we don't have to go into that aspect tonight."

Steve liked the way the Virtual Entrepreneur was laying out the concept for him, allowing it to sink in gradually without overwhelming him with too much at once.

They had left the fairways behind and were approaching the clubhouse. On their left, a rock wall meandered in and out of lush vegetation, and on the right a small brook gurgled cheerily. Steve saw silver fish jumping and flat-back turtles swimming in the glistening water.

The Virtual Entrepreneur took a practice golf swing with a phantom club as he aimed from the rough toward an open green that was about 150 yards away. The night sounds of crickets, owls, and flowing streams were truly hypnotic.

"Once I identified my three core competencies, I committed myself to further developing them," the Virtual Entrepreneur went on at last. "I studied the latest books on contemporary marketing practices that emphasized market creation and development. I learned everything I could about how to structure a network-based virtual company using win-win principles that ensured trusting and productive partner relationships. And I visited golf courses at twi-

Inset 3

The Virtual Entrepreneur's
Core Competency Ratings

Ten Major Business Strengths:	Self Ratings	Associate's Ratings	Average Ratings
1. Bottom-up marketing	10	9	9.5*
2. Strategic planning	8	7	7.5
3. Public relations and promotions	6	6	6.0
4. Deal-making and negotiations	8	9	8.5
5. Personal computer skills	5	5	5.0
6. Network and alliance building	9	10	9.5*
7. Budgeting and finance	6	5	5.5
8. Motivating people	6	7	6.5
9. Creativity and innovation	7	7	7.0
10. Understanding customer preferences	10	9	9.5*

10-Point Rating Scale:

1 = Not a Core Competency

10 = Definitely a Core Competency

* This is a Core Competency

light to better understand twilight golfers and to reflect on how I might best extend these golfers' playing time."

"And your 'eureka' to offer state-of-the-art night vision glasses to golfers tied everything together," Steve concluded. "You created a unique market, you knew exactly what type of partners to solicit, and I'm sure you were confident that enough twilight golfers, among others, would buy your product to ensure success."

The Virtual Entrepreneur was all smiles. "Bingo! Yet I must warn you that it's easy to get distracted from focusing on your core competencies at all times. For example, I could have also become heavily involved in the design stage of the night glasses instead of focusing on how to both create a novel golfing market and then organize a virtual company to quickly deliver a viable product. And designing night glasses for golfers is surely not one of my core competencies."

"So you avoided the temptation to get involved in product design."

"Absolutely." As they reached the clubhouse, the Virtual Entrepreneur stopped and turned to Steve. "Let's call it a night. I'm beat. I'll give you a call tomorrow."

"That sounds great. Thanks for all your time. I'm learning a lot."

"I'm glad to hear that," the Virtual Entrepreneur said with a smile as he shook Steve's hand. "Someday you'll be passing this along to someone else."

When Steve reached his car, he slipped off the golf spikes and put them in the trunk. Then he pulled out his personal digital assistant, settled into the front seat of his car, turned on the map light, and recorded the lessons he'd learned from this meeting.

Principle #3: Focus on Core Competencies

9. Identify your core competencies.

Members of a virtual company, whether they represent a one-person company or larger, must first list all of their key competencies. The next step is to truthfully boil the lists down to two or three core competencies which give them their major competitive advantage. A ten-point rating system can be used for both self-ratings and ratings by others who know the aspiring entrepreneur's business and management skills. The Virtual Entrepreneur's core competencies included contemporary marketing strategies, alliance building, and a deep insight into his potential customer base.

10. Dedicate nearly all of your resources to what you do best.

The Virtual Entrepreneur ensured excellence in his endeavors by excelling at his core competencies. He dedicated nearly all of his resources to the study of both contemporary marketing paradigms and large-scale deal making. He also developed a thorough understanding of his key prospective customers - frustrated twilight golfers. The Virtual Entrepreneur was committed to continually upgrading his knowledge, skills, and abilities in these three critical areas.

11. Avoid getting defocused.

The Virtual Entrepreneur knew that the pressure to defocus from his three core competencies would be great. Therefore, he vowed to always stay focused at all costs. He also knew that he could always network with new strategic partners who possessed any new skills and resources that might be required by his virtual company in the future.

12. Make sure that each partner's core competencies complement the other partners' competencies.

Virtual entrepreneurs must make sure that each partner's core competencies complement the competencies of the other members of the network. Redundancies and mismatches of competencies should always be avoided or minimized. The Virtual Entrepreneur never forgot that his virtual corporation was merely a web of strategic partners who contributed their unique core competencies to the venture.

Steve saved his notes, then put away the digital assistant. He turned off the map light and for a moment sat in darkness, thinking about the progress he'd already made. He knew that he was moving ever closer to his goal of becoming a virtual entrepreneur.

PRINCIPLE 4:
BUILD WINNING ALLIANCES

The Virtual Entrepreneur met Steve Cole at the local university's business library at 7:00 in the evening, as planned. They took a table near the library's personal computer lab.

"Steve, as always I'm glad you could make this meeting. I want to introduce you to the fourth principle of my model – building winning alliances."

"This is the lesson I've been waiting for," Steve said. He had been feeling fatigued from a stressful day at work, but now he felt his energy level rise as he anticipated this latest lesson from the Virtual Entrepreneur. "Strategic networking seemed to be at the heart of all the classic case studies you faxed to me. You have my full attention."

"The fourth principle is probably the most important. If virtual entrepreneurs are to succeed at focusing on their own core competencies while outsourcing everything else, they must be able to establish a network of cooperating partners. And outsourcing only works if world-class partners are properly selected, aligned, and integrated. Do you remember how Paul Farrow developed his web of core partners along with an expanded network of distributors? And how Ruth Owades created a streamlined network of alliances that included dependable growers and a top-tier shipper? Even Liz Greetham's electronic network formed the nervous system of her virtual operation."

"All three of these pioneering virtual entrepreneurs were able to pull together and then coordinate a network of experts," Steve said. "And they all successfully built a networked organization to rapidly transform their visions into realities."

"Yes, they did! But a critical aspect of establishing winning alliances is to always nurture a high-trust culture. Virtualpreneurs like Paul Farrow and Ruth Owades always strive to cut win-win deals with their partners to ensure that all members of their alliance feel a sense of co-destiny with the other members. Successful virtualpreneurs continuously integrate and coordinate all of their partners' activities to ensure that all members stay on schedule and contribute their fair share. This type of skillful coordination builds high levels of trust and confidence, too. The higher the sense of trust between partners, the more successful the virtual enterprise will become."

Steve asked the question that had been foremost in his mind. "How did you go about designing your own network of partners?"

"This was at the heart of my decision to become a virtual entrepreneur, Steve. The traditional approach to bringing a new product to market would be to build a full-blown research, manufacturing, and marketing company. But that was far beyond my means. I estimated that building a start-up company to design, manufacture, and market night vision sports glasses would cost in excess of two million dollars—money I definitely lacked! Yet I knew that if I forged the right strategic alliances, I could start my company for roughly one tenth of what I would spend on my own. As you can imagine, finding the right partners for those strategic alliances was critical to the success of my vision."

"Absolutely!" Steve said, nodding.

"While it isn't the intent of our meetings to elaborate on my financing strategy, I do want to describe how I went about building my web of partners."

Steve knew that if he was to ever start his own virtual company, he would have to first learn how to effectively select, align, and motivate high-quality partners. Identifying a niche opportunity, establishing a guiding vision, and identifying his own core competencies would mean nothing if he was unable to bring together a network of competent, motivated partners.

The Virtual Entrepreneur reached into his attaché case for a computer disk, then inserted it into the closest personal computer. He accessed the Microsoft PowerPoint program to show Steve a slide of his virtual organization. *(See Inset 4.)*

"This is a diagram of my own virtual enterprise–Night Vision Sports. I still get a kick out of its molecular shape. In fact, I sketched more than twenty versions of my networked company before I settled on this design. I say that only because I want you to understand the amount of conceptual effort that went into my organizational design. As you can see, all of my core partners are clearly focused on three finely delineated customer groups. I've placed myself at the upper right corner of this core network, and I consider myself to be the marketing arm. The other core members carry out research and design, manufacturing, and sales and service. I have also linked up with some secondary partners who carry out various support services such as legal and accounting activities. Finally, I have two equity investors."

Steve Cole stared intently at the slide. He was impressed with the uniqueness of this organizational design. "So you designed a virtual company in which you are personally focused on all strategic marketing and business development activities, and you contracted out everything else. Is that correct?"

"You have it, Steve. When I looked at both my major and minor areas of competency, I decided they fit nicely into the marketing realm. But I want to emphasize that I had to be very careful when selecting my core network of partners. In fact, I used this list of ten strategies to guide my efforts in selecting partners and then building strong relationships. You can never be too careful with this step. Here, you can have my copy of the list." *(See Inset 5.)*

The Virtual Entrepreneur handed Steve Cole his list of ten partnering strategies. As Steve quietly read its contents, he knew that he had just been given an important list of "Dos" and "Don'ts" that he could someday use to establish and maintain his own winning alliances.

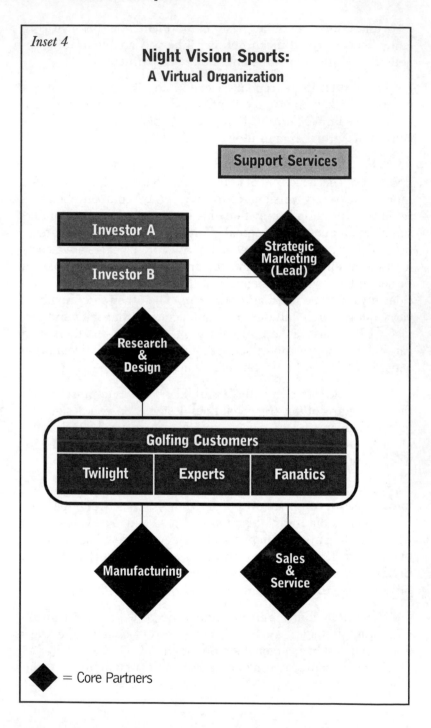

Inset 4

Night Vision Sports:
A Virtual Organization

Support Services

Investor A

Investor B

Strategic Marketing (Lead)

Research & Design

Golfing Customers

| Twilight | Experts | Fanatics |

Manufacturing

Sales & Service

◆ = Core Partners

"I religiously followed all ten of these strategies when I organized Night Vision Sports," the Virtual Entrepreneur said. "I paid special attention to points three, eight, and nine. While partner selection strategies and legal controls are very important, the ultimate success of any network is based on the lead partner's ability to build trusting relationships with the other network members. The only way this can be done is through frequent, informative, and respectful interactions with all members of the alliance."

Steve knew in his gut that what the Virtual Entrepreneur was saying was true. If all members of a network come together and form a trusting, reliable, and knowledgeable team, then the virtual enterprise would be far greater in potential than the sum of its individual parts. Steve was eager to learn all he could about the Night Vision Sports network. "Can you describe the actual members of your own network?"

"I plan to," the Virtual Entrepreneur replied with a chuckle. "But let's get some good ol' vending machine coffee first, since you look like you've had a long day. Then I'll describe the role of the key members of the Night Vision Sports network."

Core Alliance #1: The Researcher

They returned to the table with Styrofoam cups of coffee. Steve knew it would perk him up. Not that he was in danger of dozing off; the Virtual Entrepreneur was taking him into the heart of virtual entrepreneurship, and Steve was excited to hear the details.

"Steve, when I first developed my vision, I felt confident that I could effectively market night vision glasses to avid golfers," said the Virtual Entrepreneur as he settled into his chair. He set the cup carefully on the table in front of him. "Yet the typical night vision scopes and goggles used by police agencies and the military were too heavy, awkward, and uncomfortable for sports applications. Therefore, I knew I had to forge a key partnership with a technical guru who could quickly and economically redesign and modify the more traditional night vision goggles."

Inset 5

THE VIRTUAL ENTREPRENEUR'S 10 STRATEGIES FOR BUILDING STRONG ALLIANCES

Strategies to Implement:

1. Selecting partners with a record of cooperation and a history of business success.

2. Selecting partners who are committed to keeping tight control over their areas of expertise (i.e., their core competencies).

3. Seeking long-term relationships that are based on trust and mutual respect.

4. Having all partners make meaningful investments in the venture.

5. Always striving to maximize the gains of all partners.

6. Preparing tight legal contracts and self-enforcing agreements that provide strong safeguards against uncooperative, unfair, and even illegal actions.

7. Providing your partners with accurate, reliable, and comprehensive feedback on all important day-to-day, alliance-related activities.

8. Quickly responding to your partners' questions, worries, and concerns.

9. Frequently interacting with all partners on both formal and informal matters.

10. Always promoting your partners' reputations, interests, and contributions.

THE VIRTUAL ENTREPRENEUR'S 10 STRATEGIES FOR AVOIDING WEAK ALLIANCES

Practices to Avoid:

1. Choosing partners whom you know very little about.

2. Selecting partners who have no clear-cut areas of specialization and who try to be a jack-of-all-trades.

3. Seeking short-term alliances which are characterized as having little trust.

4. Utilizing partners who fail to make meaningful investments in the venture.

5. Trying to maximize your gains at the expense of your partners.

6. Failing to prepare airtight legal contracts and agreements.

7. Providing incomplete, inaccurate, or confusing feedback to partners.

8. Taking an excessively long time to respond to your partners' concerns.

9. Having infrequent and overly formal interactions.

10. Not sharing the limelight and the credit with your partners.

"So you wanted to design a technically superior product for night golfers right from the start," Steve summarized.

"Absolutely! Golfers in general are accustomed to well-designed sports equipment, so my night vision glasses had to meet their lofty expectations." The Virtual Entrepreneur paused to sip coffee and collect his thoughts. "I began my search by calling the engineering and physics departments at all of the major technical universities in the area. Nearly all of my inquiries turned out to be dead ends. Most of the engineers I spoke with exhibited an attitude of indifference, at best, toward my idea, and active discouragement at worst!"

"That must have been disappointing," Steve said. "Why did you keep moving ahead?"

The Virtual Entrepreneur smiled. "Because I am a contrarian at heart. I usually want to buy when others are selling, and create markets that others have overlooked or ignored. True entrepreneurs do not run with the pack! Also, I studied some motivational books for entrepreneurs which said that most of the truly big ideas in business were originally laughed at and ridiculed by the nonvisionary types."

Steve liked that answer. It showed real courage and perseverance. *That's the kind of entrepreneur I want to be,* he told himself. "So you took this early rejection as a cue to keep moving forward."

"Yes I did, and I strongly encourage all aspiring entrepreneurs to always rise above the naysayers. Yet there was another important issue that I had to consider when selecting my first partner. To have someone conduct this type of high-level design work could have cost me a great deal of money, so I wanted to find a talented partner who would charge me a fair rate, allow me to spread my payments over time, and most importantly, would take a major portion of his or her payment as a percentage of each pair of night vision glasses sold."

"Sounds like a tall order," Steve observed.

The Virtual Entrepreneur looked skyward with a smile, as if saying thanks. "Steve, I really lucked out...although I do believe that true entrepreneurs make their own luck by out-working and out-thinking their more complacent counterparts. My very last call put me in contact with Dr. Kodie Eastman at a technical university within twelve miles of my home. She was an astrophysicist by training, and had received the bulk of her research grants from the military. Unfortunately for her at the time, military grant funding was quickly drying up. Yet when I first met Dr. Eastman, I was impressed with how quickly she was attempting to reposition her research and design initiatives away from the sagging fortunes of the aerospace and defense industry and toward new types of consumer applications."

Steve Cole nodded thoughtfully. "So Dr. Eastman was willing to embrace your idea of taking a former military product and giving it a new identity as a type of consumer sports aid?"

"Correct! And the best part of the deal was that she had already worked as the lead consultant on military projects aimed at enhancing a soldier's night vision using the latest light-amplification technology. Dr. Eastman focused on traditional telescopes, however, and not on your typical night vision scopes. Still, we quickly struck a deal in which she offered me a discounted rate that was spread out over twelve months. She took one-third of her payment up front, one-third at the completion of the project, and the final third as a percentage of initial product sales. Dr. Eastman was obviously quite affordable, and all the details were worked out by our attorneys in a very straightforward contract that protected my ideas."

"How did you negotiate such a great deal?" Steve asked enthusiastically. *I'll want to do some creative deal-making for my own virtual enterprise,* he thought.

"As I mentioned, Dr. Eastman wanted to shift her focus from military to consumer applications. She wanted to redirect her research and design focus, while I wanted to redirect a product's application. I approached Dr. Eastman at the perfect time in her consulting practice to make this type of deal. Also, Dr. Eastman viewed the money she would be receiving more as a supplement to her main income, since she already had a stable job as a well-respected academic professor. The bottom line was that Dr.

Eastman really wasn't seeking a ton of money. I believe that she both respected and bought into my vision, and she even signed a non-compete contract to acknowledge that the original idea was mine."

Steve was truly impressed with the Virtual Entrepreneur's first strategic partner. "I experienced your Night Hawk 2000s, so I know she delivered her end of the bargain. What was the key to her quick success?"

"There were a few keys. First, she was definitely an expert in the field of electronically augmenting night vision. Second, we purchased five different types of military night vision goggles and identified product dimensions and features that would have to be modified and tweaked to give us a superior sports product. Third, she had access to some brilliant graduate students who helped her to quickly develop a working prototype. This allowed us to re-think a few of our features before we sent the prototype on to manu-facturing. And finally," the Virtual Entrepreneur added with a broad smile, "Dr. Eastman is a nine-handicap golfer who felt that she would have even more time to improve her game if she could play at night."

Core Alliance #2: The Manufacturer

It was getting late. Steve Cole and the Virtual Entrepreneur had moved their conversation to the library's lounge. The lounge chairs were more comfortable and much closer to the coffee vend-ing machines.

The Virtual Entrepreneur moved to the edge of his chair as he began to describe his second core alliance. His hands were clasped in front of him.

"Signing up my second partner was extremely challenging and required keen skills of negotiation on my part. I knew that I could never afford to manufacture any significant volume of Night Hawk 2000s with my capital budget. Therefore, I had to form the perfect strategic alliance to transform my product design into a tangible reality."

"You seem to have grown a little more tense describing the formation of this partnership," Steve observed. "Is that a fair statement?"

This earned a thin smile. "It is definitely fair. I knew that the success or failure of my virtual company could rest on this step. I had to sign up a manufacturer who had the expertise, time, equipment, and staff to produce my Night Hawks. Yet I also knew that the manufacturer would have to produce the first 200 pairs mostly on a handshake and credit alone, since I did not have enough capital to cover the full production costs."

"Sounds like a challenge, all right," Steve acknowledged.

"All entrepreneurs must be able to overcome nerve-wracking hurdles if they are to ever succeed."

"How did you pull off this deal?"

"I did a thorough background check on the five companies that developed the night scopes that Dr. Eastman and I initially examined. Three of those companies were on the East Coast, so I immediately ruled them out. Another company was fortunate enough to receive an expanded government contract and did not have any excess capacity.

"I discovered that the fifth company, called Advanced Systems and Technologies, or AST, was housed within forty miles of my favorite oceanside golf course. More specifically, it was located in a secluded research complex close to the Navy's West Coast submarine research center. I did some additional background research and discovered that AST's president, Melany Ford, was a graduate of the California Institute of Technology. She dual-majored in applied electronics and physics. I had a strong hunch that Melany would become the key partner in my network. I was committed to signing her up."

"To accomplish that, first you had to get her interested in your project—to accept your guiding vision, I guess you could say—and then you had to negotiate some win-win terms."

"Exactly! When I first visited Melany Ford at AST, I knew her company had manufactured tens of thousands of traditional night vision scopes for the Navy over the past ten years. Those figures came from a government report that was available to the public over the Internet. Yet I also noticed that the average number of night vision scopes produced by her company over the past three years dropped 35% from the previous seven years. This analysis strongly suggested that AST had idle production capacity that could be immediately directed toward Night Vision Sports. In fact, AST was a prime candidate to take on custom work from the outside." The Virtual Entrepreneur leaned back in his chair, took a sip of coffee, and then made one more point. "As an aside, Melany informed me that her husband was a talented one-handicap golfer. He regularly played in such tournaments as the California Amateur Match Play Classic and even the U.S. Amateur Golf Championship. I have this strange feeling that Melany initially listened to my sales pitch just so she would be able to learn about an exciting new golf product that she could share with her husband."

Steve Cole chuckled. "So you lucked out again with one of your golf connections. Not only did AST have the idle capacity, it also had a leader who had an indirect interest in golf."

The Virtual Entrepreneur nodded thoughtfully. "Well…was it really luck? Or was this another example of synchronicity that I was benefitting from?"

Steve smiled. He liked these little philosophical remarks. "Maybe you're right! So tell me, how did you close the deal."

"I had to do my homework first, of course," the Virtual Entrepreneur replied. "I learned that approximately 50% of AST's $72 million per year in revenues came from portable military radar systems, 40% came from the development of night scopes, and the other revenue came from service contracts and special research projects. That information came right from AST's annual and quarterly reports. Since revenues related to night vision scopes were down 30%, AST definitely had capacity sitting idle. I felt sure that the company would jump at the chance to rebuild its night scopes business by adding custom projects from outside sources."

"So you really made a good decision when you zeroed in on AST. Obviously, the company met your selection criteria."

"Yes it did! Melany Ford typically conducted business by charging a customer for the cost of the expensive prototype, along with any special production equipment she might need. She then expected payment upon delivery of the first products off the production line. Melany would also offer quantity discounts for large run orders. Yet Melany was flexible enough to deviate from this approach when she decided to engage in custom work with Night Vision Sports." Steve could see the look of gratitude in the Virtual Entrepreneur's eyes as he said this.

"How did she modify her approach?" Steve asked.

"Melany knew that charging me a large sum up front would prevent me from getting into this line of business. It would also deny AST a promising customer. Melany also knew that she and I shared both a common risk and a common interest. So the two of us worked together to rewrite the rules. We took a joint risk!"

Steve didn't miss the Virtual Entrepreneur's point. Risk-taking was still one of the most important traits of aspiring entrepreneurs. Steve knew that he would face his own set of risks when he launched his virtual company.

"Entrepreneurs must be daring, Steve. I thank God that Melany Ford still retained her entrepreneurial spirit. Instead of just quoting me a price, she and her attorney negotiated a win-win agreement in which AST would share a large portion of the start-up costs with me. And instead of charging me a prohibitive cost for the first run of Night Hawk 2000s, and then having the cost of subsequent runs drop off from there according to the size of my orders, Melany agreed to spread AST's costs over the life of the initial product run. She was great!"

"I can see that her cooperation really lowered your financial barrier to entry. Now I know why this is one of your key alliances."

"I believe that Melany ultimately entered this agreement because she respected my practical marketing skills and she knew I had a novel idea. She also felt that I had the vision and persistence to grow Night Vision Sports for our mutual benefit. But most importantly, Melany trusted me when I promised to focus on my own core competencies and not interfere with her company's manufacturing process."

Steve reflected on this. "You respected her position as the manufacturing expert, and she must have sensed your total confidence in her company. It sounds like a case of mutual trust and respect."

"Correct! What Melany was really banking on was anticipated volume. She had her own independent market research firm conduct a study which showed that at the $2,000 to $3,000 price range, I could probably sell a minimum of 2,000 units in my first year, 3,000 the second year, and then continue to grow my unit sales by 50% for each of the first five years. Melany figured she could recoup her startup costs after the first 200 units were sold. Moreover, Melany figured she could use this strategic relationship to document to her shareholders that she was successfully reducing her dependency on military funding. She could take this kind of news to the bank and borrow against it if she ever needed to."

The Virtual Entrepreneur had made his point that AST was also benefitting from the alliance. Steve could see that this would be an important theme in any virtual enterprise. The negotiated deals between partners had to be win-win deals for all of them. But another question had occurred to Steve. "Weren't you concerned that AST would take your unique idea and run with it?"

"That was a risk I chose to take. At that point, my attorney already had a patent pending on the Night Hawk 2000s, but I didn't even need to mention that. And I didn't ask Melany Ford to sign a non-disclosure or non-compete form up front. If I had, she probably wouldn't have taken the time to hear my plan. After I shared my idea with her, she acknowledged to me that she had been a little myopic in her own thinking and never thought about promoting her company's night vision scopes in a sports market. Besides, she was smart enough to realize that AST did not have the proper marketing mechanism to make that work. In brief, Melany realized that she had more to learn and gain by working with a strategic partner like myself than by trying to emulate me."

The Virtual Entrepreneur went on to explain that the agreement between AST and Night Vision Sports was only five pages long, even though both sides had their attorneys review it. AST had an escape clause in case the Virtual Entrepreneur did not realize his anticipated sales volume. And if the two parties ever split up, each would be barred for three years from entering the other's business. Finally, both Melany Ford and the Virtual Entrepreneur could mutually agree to extend their partnership, which originally covered five years.

Steve Cole was impressed. The Virtual Entrepreneur had succeeded in negotiating a flexible, win-win contract with AST. Both parties had a clear understanding of what they needed to do to move forward once they signed the document.

"Thanks for explaining your second alliance in so much detail," Steve said gratefully.

"You're welcome!" the Virtual Entrepreneur said cheerfully, slapping a hand on Steve's shoulder. "I think that's enough for today. Tomorrow I'll introduce you to a member of my sales and service network. Let's meet at the Dry Gulch Golf Resort at 9:00 p.m. I want you to meet my number one sales rep, golf professional Jack Palmer. And bring your clubs!"

Core Alliance #3: The Distributor

Jack Palmer's pro shop was bustling with activity despite the fact that it was dark outside except for some illumination from a half moon. Steve Cole could smell the French roast coffee that Jack had brewed for the eight golfers in his pro shop.

The two foursomes stepped outside to tee off, and both the Virtual Entrepreneur and Steve smiled as all of the golfers put on their Night Hawk 2000s and then flipped on their power switches.

"Golfers enter a different world when they play this course at night," Jack Palmer said. "They see geometrically patterned reptiles, glistening rocks, desert palms, and beautiful orange-green cloud patterns. I wish I had the time to join them."

"Maybe you could join Steve Cole and me for a round later," the Virtual Entrepreneur suggested. "Steve is a friend of mine who's studying how our distributor network sells night vision glasses."

"Glad to meet you," Jack said, shaking Steve's hand. "I'm honored to be a member of the Night Vision Sports network. What would you like to know?" It was already clear to Steve that Jack Palmer felt a sense of co-destiny with the other members of the network.

"It's an honor to meet you, Jack. The Virtual Entrepreneur told me that you were his number one distributor. How did you achieve such status?"

Jack smiled. "Let me back up a bit and explain how I first got involved with this product. I'm a member of the Northern California Professional Golfer's Association, and I chair the NCPGA's section for club professionals. About two years ago, the Virtual Entrepreneur made a powerful presentation to 128 NCPGA club professionals. He described how he wanted to create a network of professionals to distribute what he believed to be an exciting and revolutionary new golf product, which he referred to as his Night Hawk 2000s. The Virtual Entrepreneur was both articulate and enthusiastic about his Night Hawks, and he definitely aroused my interest!"

Steve addressed his next question to the Virtual Entrepreneur. "So you initially focused on a targeted group of club professionals as your distributors."

"Right," the Virtual Entrepreneur confirmed. "I explained the unique niche that my night vision glasses filled and how they might fit into the typical club professional's product mix. Then I gave club professionals an elegant brochure that could be used to introduce this product to their golfing clientele. Finally, I had brought 150 pairs of Night Hawks with me. I gave the pros a quick lesson in how to use them, then offered to let them use the glasses for fifteen days, free of charge."

Again, Steve was impressed by the Virtual Entrepreneur's approach. He had obviously given careful consideration to how he should handle this important step as he put together his virtual company.

"Let me tell you exactly what went through my head at the time," Jack interjected. "First, I knew I could get more golf shop sales if I could extend my golfers' playing time. I would simply hire a part-timer to cover the extra golf shop hours. Second, it was clear to me that the Virtual Entrepreneur had done his research, since he knew that the typical club pro could not afford to enter a wholesale-retail model with the high-priced night vision glasses. Therefore, he offered a hefty 15% commission. This came to almost $450 for each pair of Night Hawks that I sold. I don't make that kind of profit from the golf club sets I sell, so I had no problem being paid a commission like a sales rep. Finally, and without exaggeration, I wanted a pair of these special glasses myself so I could play at night. Club professionals never have enough time to play golf."

"Let me add a few more points," the Virtual Entrepreneur said. "I could afford to offer a 15% commission for one reason: I kept my costs down with my virtual organization. I signed up 78% of the pros on the spot. They could see that they had nothing to lose, and they didn't want their golfing buddies to gain more practice time than themselves. In addition, the club pros have become such a successful distribution channel that I am seriously considering expanding my operation down the state of California within six months, and I'll further expand my network of club pro dealers as I begin to move east."

"Wow!" Steve exclaimed as the full impact of this dawned on him. "If you sold 2,000 pairs of Night Hawks in just over a year using only a Northern California network, the sky seems to be the limit as you move down the state and then east."

"The Virtual Entrepreneur found a way to reduce the limitations of darkness imposed by the nighttime sky," Jack Palmer said with a hearty chuckle. "But listen, I'm going to be heading home now. Why don't you guys go ahead and tee off without me. It was a pleasure meeting you, Steve."

Steve and the Virtual Entrepreneur decided to play only nine holes of golf that evening. Steve had upgraded his golf set to include three oversized metal woods: the one-wood, the three-wood, and the five-wood. His drive on the first hole went right down the middle of the fairway. It left an echoing sound of a high-compression golf ball hitting a hollow, high-tech metal-headed driver. However, the 225-yard drive was too low for night golf, and it was slowed by the nighttime dew on the first fairway.

In contrast, the Virtual Entrepreneur hit a power fade that flew about 275 yards in the air but did not get any roll. He had only a half wedge shot left into this 375-yard dogleg right.

As they were leisurely walking down the first fairway and enjoying the peaceful nighttime visions around them, the Virtual Entrepreneur continued his lesson on how to establish winning alliances.

"Steve, I've introduced you to the core members of my network. I'm very proud of them. And as you might remember from my organizational diagram, all of the core members stay focused on our three major categories of customers at all times: (1) the after-work twilight golfers, (2) the expert golfers who want more time to play and practice, and (3) the fanatics who would use any excuse or fad to be able to play golf at night. My four secondary partners complete my network." The Virtual Entrepreneur stopped talking as Steve Cole hit a solid seven iron to within three feet of the green. The Virtual Entrepreneur hit a punch wedge shot to within five feet of the pin.

"So you conceptualized Night Vision Sports as consisting of both core and secondary network members," Steve summarized.

"Correct, although I treat all of my partners with equal amounts of respect and support. My support staff includes Sally Lynch, my accountant, and Ben Mason, my attorney. I have known these two professionals since my college days, and they charge me very fair rates. Plus, I only pay them when I use them."

Steve nodded. "That beats having a corporate accountant and lawyer on staff or on a retainer."

"Absolutely. And when I need additional support, such as the patent attorney or a tax accountant, Ben and Sally know who to get. A golden rule for all virtual entrepreneurs is to always keep costs down and keep the organization as simple as possible." The

Virtual Entrepreneur gestured toward Steve's ball. "Chip up on the green and let's putt out. I'll describe my final two partners after we finish our nine holes. For now, let's play some golf and enjoy this beautiful evening."

After finishing their nine holes, Steve and the Virtual Entrepreneur returned to the golf shop and waved to Jack Palmer's part-timer, who was cleaning clubs. The Virtual Entrepreneur immediately suggested that he and Steve sit down next to the warm fireplace. He handed Steve a tangy cup of French roast. Then he began to describe the financial dimension of his network – his two investors.

"I relied on a few strategies to reduce my dependence on outside investors, Steve. First, I had saved about $100,000 in cash over the years, and I was willing to use bootstrap financing to launch my company. My philosophy was that for the most part, outside investors can hinder an entrepreneur's progress. Some are too insecure about their investments, and they tend to meddle in the day-to-day operations in an attempt to ensure a high return. So I wanted to keep outside investors to a minimum."

"I can see why," Steve said, nodding.

"My goal was to raise $200,000 in total capital to get my virtual company launched. I included that amount in my business plan, and it was based on the assumption that I could cut deals with my core partners that would dramatically reduce my startup costs for things like research and design, product development, and sales."

Again, Steve nodded. The Virtual Entrepreneur had just summarized one of the major benefits of a virtual enterprise–cost containment. Steve realized that as he learned more about the Virtual Entrepreneur's own business, he was becoming more and more eager to get started on his own.

"I already had $100,000 from my savings. I approached Ross Paris, my community banker, for a $25,000 loan that was collateralized by my home and personal savings."

"So Investor A was a commercial banker," Steve reflected. "Who was Investor B?"

"I took another approach with my second investor, since I still needed $75,000. I had learned from my readings that a type of private investor called an 'angel' was more likely to loan money to startup companies like mine, as opposed to venture capitalists or public or private companies. Therefore, I subscribed to an online service that allowed me to describe the deal I was offering, and the service searched for private investors or 'angels' who were looking for that type of equity investment. I hit pay dirt after only one day of online searching."

"That's impressive!" Steve Cole said. "Who in the world did you find so quickly?"

"I can't tell you her name, Steve. She wants to remain an anonymous investor. Let me just say she is one of the top touring golfers in the Ladies Professional Golf Association. Her investment allowed me to reach the $200,000 that I needed to launch my virtual enterprise."

"So with that, you've covered four of the five principles of virtual entrepreneurship," Steve said. He ticked them off on his fingers as he summarized. "You identified a niche opportunity by finding a way to let golfers play regulation courses after dark. You established a guiding vision to clarify the purpose and direction of Night Vision Sports. You identified your own core competencies and relied on others for everything else. And you negotiated winning alliances with partners." Steve paused to think. "As I recall, your fifth principle relates to familiarity with computers and information technology."

"Right," the Virtual Entrepreneur said, nodding. "It's easy to gain, and then to quickly lose, competitive advantage if you don't stay at the cutting edge of business technology." He smiled. "But staying there on the crest of the wave can be fun! Let's have lunch tomorrow at the Cyber-Café. I can't wait to show you another facet of Night Vision Sports."

Steve readily agreed, and the Virtual Entrepreneur offered to pick him up at his office at 11:00.

As he drove home, Steve thought about everything he had learned from the Virtual Entrepreneur. Tomorrow the Virtual Entrepreneur would tell him about the final principle, and their frequent meetings would be coming to an end. But he knew that their relationship had deepened into friendship, and for that he was grateful.

Steve was tired when he got home. But before he went to bed, he booted up his computer to record the lessons he had just learned about how to establish winning alliances.

Principle #4: Build Winning Alliances

13. Design a network of strategic partners.

The Virtual Entrepreneur went through twenty different organizational designs before he settled on a molecular design that included, not counting himself, three core partners, two professional staff members, and two investors. Interestingly, his "molecular design" is slightly different from the "hard-wired" designs used by such virtual entrepreneurs as Liz Greetham at Weiss, Peck & Greer Venture Partners, and Jeff and Mary Freeman at Front Porch Computers. Greetham and the Freemans relied more on online computer link-ups.

14. Select only the best and the brightest to form the network.

The Virtual Entrepreneur selected a talented group of professionals whom he could entrust with his vision. He chose people who specialized in specific aspects of his project. His fine-tuned selection strategy significantly increased his company's chances of success. For example, technical professionals who had previous experience with night vision instruments made ideal designers and manufacturers. Club pros formed an ideal sales distribution channel.

15. Negotiate win-win deals which give all partners a sense of co-destiny.

The Virtual Entrepreneur was a subtle yet highly effective negotiator. He convinced his strategic partners to buy into his dream, and then he offered them a deal that would minimize his startup costs yet prove lucrative to his partners down the road. His partners trusted him and had faith in his virtual enterprise. They also liked golf!

16. Focus the core network on the customers.

Finally, the Virtual Entrepreneur knew that he had to focus his core network on his targeted group of potentially lucrative customers. This tight focus is clearly illustrated in his organizational diagram. In addition, he chose partners, including a key investor, who all knew something about golf. This was probably no accident and helped to ensure that his network would be deeply sensitive to his customers' needs.

PRINCIPLE 5:
EMBRACE ELECTRONIC COMMERCE

The Virtual Entrepreneur was in a particularly ebullient mood when he picked up Steve the next day. After his morning workout on the treadmill and a refreshing shower, Steve was eager for another adventure in virtual entrepreneurship.

"Today will be a special treat, Steve!" the Virtual Entrepreneur said as he merged his car into traffic and headed toward the Cyber-Café. "I know you'll enjoy it, because I already know that you appreciate the way today's technology can give the entrepreneur a competitive edge."

"You're right!" Steve agreed. The Virtual Entrepreneur's sparkling enthusiasm was contagious. "I'm eager to hear all about day-to-day technology applications of virtual entrepreneurship. I've seen how you rely on your cellphone, digital assistant, and laptop computer to create a mobile office experience."

The Virtual Entrepreneur nodded. "Like any road warrior entrepreneur, I started out with a bare-boned technology strategy. I switched from a desktop computer to a laptop so I could become part of the mobile workforce. I also made sure that I mastered a handful of the most useful small business software, including word processing and financial spreadsheets. I even mastered a user-friendly database management program to keep track of my partners' production and distribution schedules, and to analyze the purchasing patterns of my customers." He paused as he alertly navigated a challenging intersection. "My favorite software is a desktop publishing program which allows me to quickly publish color handouts and brochures that I can use in a wide variety of sales and marketing presentations. I really have fun with that!"

"I'm sure you use E-mail to stay in touch with your network of business partners."

"Of course! In fact, I took this a step further and asked all of my partners and distributors to install a groupware communications package so all of us could participate in virtual team meetings. I don't have videoconferencing cameras mounted on their personal computers yet, but that's just around the corner."

Steve was impressed with the Virtual Entrepreneur's strategy of incrementally improving his virtual company's technology infrastructure and applications. "Do your partners like the groupware?"

The Virtual Entrepreneur chuckled. "They love it! The only problem is, once they saw what it could do for them, they wanted even more! Believe me, I won't have any trouble keeping my partners on the leading edge of technology."

"Good! So what's in store for today?"

The Virtual Entrepreneur brought his car to a smooth stop in front of the Cyber-Café, then pulled neatly into a parking space. He turned off the engine and looked over at Steve. "My friend, you are about to become one of the first people to see the next incarnation of Night Vision Sports' technology infrastructure!"

The Cyber-Café was housed in a modern chrome building with green-tinted windows. The Virtual Entrepreneur told Steve that a techno-savvy crowd of Generation X'ers frequented the restaurant in order to log onto the Internet during their lunch breaks.

Inside, Steve saw a row of gray, oval-shaped marble tables. Mounted on the corner of each table was a black portable network computer with a high-resolution color monitor.

"I've never used one of these network PC's before," Steve said, "but I've read that they're an inexpensive way to log onto the Internet."

"Network PC's are extremely cost efficient for people who just want to surf the Internet. They're also very user friendly! I like to spend my lunch hours surfing the Web for business tips and competitive intelligence." The Virtual Entrepreneur gestured toward a table that had just been vacated. "Let's grab that corner table so we can log onto the Internet."

He's like a little boy getting ready to try out a shiny new bicycle! Steve thought, unable to stop himself from grinning. *I wonder what new and exciting element of virtual entrepreneurship we're going to explore.*

After seating themselves, they looked over the lunch menu. Steve was surprised to see that the menu only contained a wide variety of health shakes. Then he realized that serving greasy hamburgers and fries wouldn't cut it when patrons were going to be using the restaurant's network PC's.

When the waiter came to their table, the Virtual Entrepreneur ordered first. "I'll have a blueberry-banana power shake with a scoop of protein powder and Vitamin C." He folded the menu and looked over at Steve. "Have you decided what you'd like for lunch?"

Steve nodded. "I'll have the orange-pineapple shake with a scoop of the crushed mental alertness vitamin pack." Steve felt a bit like a character in William Gibson's novel *Neuromancer.*

After the waiter had gone, the Virtual Entrepreneur turned to the computer. "Now we'll have some fun!" His gaze was fixed on the monitor as he clicked on a globe-shaped icon labeled *The World Wide Web.* He was heading directly to cyberspace.

Steve leaned forward for a better look at the screen. "What Web sites are we gunning for?"

The Virtual Entrepreneur carefully typed in a universal resource locator address, then turned to Steve. "When I hit the *Enter* key, we'll be taking a little trip, Steve."

"A trip?" Steve looked around the cafe. "Is this place going to blast off into outer space? Or is Scotty waiting in the control booth to beam us up?"

The Virtual Entrepreneur laughed. "We'll be taking a *virtual* trip. We're going to Night Vision Sports' Virtual Golf Shop!"

Steve's eyes widened in surprise. "Your...Virtual Golf Shop?"

"Absolutely! Steve, do you have any idea how many people shop the Internet nowadays?"

Steve thought for a moment, then shook his head. "Quite a few, I suppose. I buy office supplies and books from Internet stores."

"More than 70 million Americans are surfing the Web, and more than nine million shop online. That's a lot of potential customers! Of course, we've barely scratched the surface of its potential. Predictions are for more than $100 billion in online sales by the year 2000, and over $300 billion by 2002."

"Wow!" Steve exclaimed. "I had no idea it was growing that fast."

"Not only that, but Internet shoppers are good customers. They're well-educated and they have more income than the average American. They're spending a lot of time online, too – nearly half are online daily."

"I'll bet a lot of them are golfers, too!" Steve added with a smile.

The Virtual Entrepreneur laughed. "You'd win that bet, Steve. I'm thrilled to be a part of E-commerce. It's an exciting new use of today's technology. Entrepreneurs like Michael Dell of Dell Computer Corporation are proving just how successful and profitable it can be. It's changing the way companies sell their products and services."

"From your enthusiasm, I assume you believe that E-commerce will work well for Night Vision Sports."

"I'm *sure* of it, Steve. In order to get the word out about my night vision glasses, I've used traditional promotional methods such as direct mail campaigns and advertisements in golf magazines. Most sales have come from recommendations of golf pros or word of mouth. Those methods have certainly generated some impressive sales numbers.

"Then I realized that I couldn't possibly offer my night vision products on a global or even national basis without establishing an electronic commerce Web site." His smile broadened. "Today is the grand opening of my Web site. It'll reach millions of shoppers every day, and my cost will be about $100 a month."

"That *is* impressive." Steve scooted his chair closer to the monitor. "All right, let's go on that trip!"

Before the Virtual Entrepreneur could press the *Enter* key, the waiter returned with their shakes. Steve was so excited, he'd almost forgotten about lunch.

After they had both taken a sip of their shakes, the Virtual Entrepreneur grinned and made a dramatic gesture of tapping his index finger on the *Enter* key. A Web page began loading. The first image to catch Steve's eye was that of a sleek, stylish pair of Night Hawk 2000s gleaming silver against a tranquil backdrop of blues and greens. Across the top of the page was the smoky black lettering identifying Night Vision Sports. Steve was immediately impressed with the combination of simplicity and beauty.

"Very nice!" he murmured.

As he began to assimilate other details of the Web page, he saw that a strip along the left side was separated from the rest by a dark border. The background of that strip was light brown. At the top, in crisp white lettering, was an E-mail address and an 800 number for Night Vision Sports. Below that were several page links, and Steve smiled when he saw that the link icons resembled golf greens, complete with numbered flags.

"I like the design," Steve said. "It's simple, and the coloring is nice. Brown, blue, and green—the colors of a golf course."

"I want to make my guests feel right at home," said the Virtual Entrepreneur. "And one thing I know about them is that they like golf."

"The Night Hawks are beautiful! They look very high-tech there in the middle of all those soft greens and blues." Under the image of the night vision glasses were two buttons labeled *Tell Me More* and *The Nighttime Golf Experience*. Steve's eyes moved back to the icons on the left side of the screen. The first was labeled *The Virtual Golf Shop*. Below were icons labeled *Ask the Pro, Nighttime Golf Courses, About Night Vision Sports, Guest Book,* and *The Virtual Country Club.* "I can see that you've gone well beyond selling your night vision glasses."

"My Virtual Golf Shop sells many products," the Virtual Entrepreneur said. "But I wanted to sell more than just tangible products. In fact, I had two other strategic goals in mind when I designed my Web site. First, I wanted to develop an online community of night golfers. And second, I wanted to offer information-based golfing services that would serve as a magnet to ensure that my guests want to keep coming back. One key to that is that my guests must feel as if they're in control of their own interactive experience."

Steve's eyes went to the last icon on the screen. "You've even got a Virtual Country Club?"

"Sure! Let's take a look." The Virtual Entrepreneur clicked on that icon, and they were taken to another attractive page with several images of golfers in various poses and settings. Prominently displayed were three icons labeled *Tour the Country Club, Join Now,* and *Members Only.* The Virtual Entrepreneur clicked on the *Members Only* icon, then entered a password which brought up yet another page. "For only $98 per year, I'll be able to provide all of the member-only services listed on the screen."

As Steve examined the services that were offered, the Virtual Entrepreneur explained how it worked. First, members would have access to a twenty-four-hours-a-day, seven-days-a-week online chat room that would be frequented by other nighttime golfers. There were also areas where they could post questions or comments about nighttime golf, to learn about courses that have nighttime hours, and even to meet and chat with other nighttime golfers online. A member could also establish a golf handicap based totally on rounds of nighttime golf. These handicaps would be updated on a weekly basis.

"I see this as the electronic version of the 19th hole," the Virtual Entrepreneur said. "As I said, I want to offer more than products on my Web site. I want it to be a pleasant, interactive experience. My ultimate goal is to create a tight-knit virtual community of nighttime golfers. My guests can share stories about both the beauty and the challenges of nighttime golf. They'll also receive a directory of all the worldwide courses that offer nighttime golf, and they can even make their tee time reservations on this Web site. Plus, they'll get discounts on many of the products available in the Virtual Golf Shop."

"Can we take a look at that?"

"Of course!" The Virtual Entrepreneur moved the mouse pointer to the left side of the screen and clicked on the icon labeled *The Virtual Golf Shop.* Steve realized that all of the navigation links on the left side of the screen had remained in place even as the Virtual Entrepreneur brought up other pages on the main area of the screen. That would make navigation extremely easy.

Now the screen displayed images of products ranging from glow balls to waterproof golf shoes, and even golf-related video games. Steve saw listings for golf clubs that provided higher trajectory golf shots, making them ideal for the dew-covered fairways that accompany nighttime golf. The Virtual Entrepreneur was offering a much broader line of complementary products on the Web. Across the top of this page were transaction-related icons labeled *Add to My Cart, View Cart,* and *Check Out.*

"I'm assuming that visitors to your site will simply click on the products they want to get more details. Then they can add the product to an electronic shopping cart, and then the online sale will be completed via a secure credit card transaction."

"You are almost correct," the Virtual Entrepreneur said with a smile. "The selected products will be added to a virtual *golf* cart rather than a shopping cart. For anyone ordering Night Hawks, we'll E-mail or fax them a brief form to be completed by their optometrist so the lenses of their night glasses will be perfectly refracted for them."

"Now *that's* a great idea!" Steve said. His eyes returned to the narrow strip on the left side of the screen, and the icon labeled *About Night Vision Sports.* "You've even got information about your company."

"I want my guests to feel as if they know who they're dealing with. I give them a complete history of Night Vision Sports, and I've included some testimonials from satisfied users of my Night Hawks." The Virtual Entrepreneur paused. "Come to think of it, I don't think I've ever encountered a dissatisfied customer!

"And there's one more service that I offer—my referral service. I didn't forget my sales partners, the golf professionals. I will refer site guests to them for special nighttime golf lessons. In addition, some of my guests will want a list of pro shops where they can rent Night Hawks instead of buying them. I'm hoping that all of my strategic partners will be big winners based on the success of my Web site!"

Steve suddenly remembered his power shake, which he hadn't touched after the first sip. After drinking a few swallows, he said, "I notice that you refer to visitors to your site as *guests*. Do you mind telling me why?"

"Not at all," said the Virtual Entrepreneur. "But let me ask *you* a question. When you invite guests to your home, do you go out of your way to make them feel welcome?"

"Sure! Since I invited them, I think it's my responsibility to make sure they have a good time and that they feel comfortable being there."

"Exactly!" the Virtual Entrepreneur said. "You've just answered your own question."

Steve thought about that, then realized what the Virtual Entrepreneur was telling him. "You want to think of every person who visits your Web site as a guest. You want to make sure they feel comfortable and have a good time while they're there."

"Right! There are several ways to make sure they have a good time. One way is to keep each page of your Web site as simple as possible. If guests were coming to your home for dinner, you would probably make sure there wasn't a lot of clutter lying around. Web sites shouldn't be cluttered, either. The navigation links on the home page should be very clear, easy to read, and easy to understand. Your guests should feel secure and comfortable with their ability to get around quickly. I want my virtual storefront to be so inviting that my guests will want to keep going so they can find out more about my products. That's one of the main principles about Internet stores: make it easy for the shopper to get the information he needs and to find the product he wants. Then make it easy for him to buy it."

"It couldn't be easier than this," Steve said, his eyes still fixed on the screen. "Can we go back to the home page for a moment?"

"Sure." The Virtual Entrepreneur clicked on the *Home* icon.

Steve indicated the icon labeled *Tell Me More* under the image of the Night Hawk 2000's. "I assume you've put all the detail about the night vision glasses there, so it wouldn't clutter up the front page."

"You're learning fast, Steve! Information on that page includes the price, how to order, available accessories, and so on."

"I'm impressed!" Steve said, leaning back at last. "Did you design this Web site yourself?"

"Most of it," the Virtual Entrepreneur said, clearly pleased with Steve's reaction. "I came up with the concept and the general layout, but I hired a pro to construct the site itself. That part definitely wasn't in my list of core competencies!"

"There must be a lot of strategic decisions to make when setting up a virtual storefront on the Internet," Steve said.

"More than I could have imagined! Besides creating a pleasant, effective storefront, you have to decide how to process orders and payments and how to market the site. You probably noticed that I have an icon for *Guest Book* prominently displayed on the front page. I wanted to make it easy for guests to sign the book and leave their E-mail addresses. That will give me potential buyers for new products. I need to learn more about how to effectively capture all customer contact information and then critically analyze it in order to optimally understand my customers. For example, I may ask my guests to complete an online questionnaire that reflects their buying preferences.

"I also had to make sure my Web site would be easy to find. My domain name is **www.nightvisionsports.com**. Anyone who has seen my company's logo in a golf magazine or a flyer in a golf shop will have a good chance of finding me with the straightforward address. Of course, I've also registered with all the major search engines." The Virtual Entrepreneur leaned back away from the keyboard and reached for his health shake. "Let's finish lunch. Then I want to show you one more feature of my Web site."

After finishing their shakes, both Steve and the Virtual Entrepreneur scooted their chairs closer to the computer monitor.

"I think you'll like this," the Virtual Entrepreneur said as he clicked on the icon labeled *The Nighttime Golf Experience.* Within seconds, Steve found himself looking out through a pair of Night Hawks as a golfer played a course at night.

"That's the 18th hole at Pebble Beach," the Virtual Entrepreneur said.

"Yes, I thought so," Steve murmured, entranced by the scene unfolding in front of him. The video clip had been shot from the perspective of how this famous course looked through the night vision glasses. The course was emerald green, and the ocean waves could be heard beating against the coastline. The nighttime golfer even enjoyed looking at a herd of Pacific whales under the ghostly glow of moonlight.

"This should definitely stimulate sales!" Steve blurted out in excitement as it ended. "I don't know how any golfer worth his salt could watch that and not immediately click to the Virtual Golf Shop and place an order!"

The Virtual Entrepreneur chuckled at Steve's enthusiasm. "Thanks, Steve. This is absolutely the quickest, easiest way to share the experience of nighttime golf with millions of golfers worldwide. Now you can see why I'm so enthusiastic about E-commerce." The Virtual Entrepreneur reached into his shirt pocket and took out a single folded piece of paper, which he handed to Steve. "Here's one more list of the more contemporary virtualpreneurs to add to your file. I've described a few of the more successful retail Web sites that provide instant access to online product information, along with cost-effective distribution. These sites also provide customer service and technical support twenty-four hours a day, seven days a week. I encourage you to visit and study these Web sites and others as you continue your studies on electronic commerce." *(See inset 6.)*

"Thank you." Steve felt almost overwhelmed with excitement about everything he had seen and heard during this meeting with the Virtual Entrepreneur. "Can I have a few minutes to write some notes?"

"Of course," said the Virtual Entrepreneur graciously. "Take all the time you need."

Steve got out his personal digital assistant and wrote the following notes. He would then make plans for a final meeting to say goodbye to the Virtual Entrepreneur.

Inset 6
Illustrative E-Commerce Web Sites

Company #1: Virtual Vineyards

Web Address: www.virtualvin.com

Description: This multimillion-dollar online retailer special-izes in gourmet foods and obscure wines from family-owned vineyards in California and Europe. The company was founded in 1994. Sales have been multiplying by 10 to 15 percent every month. Online customers hail from over 50 countries. The ripest international market is Japan.

Company #2: 1-800-Flowers

Web Address: www.1800flowers.com

Description: This virtual enterprise specializes in the online sales of floral products and gifts. This site generates millions of dollars in revenues per year, driven by an astonishing 2.5 million Web site hits per day! This virtual company's goal is to continually satisfy its online customers by offering conve-nience, customer service, and high quality floral and gifting products in a virtual environment that emulates a brick and mortar retail store.

Company #3: eSchwab

Web Address: www.eschwab.com

Description: This is the fast-growing online investment division of Charles Schwab, one of the largest discount brokers. The eSchwab division is a market share leader. Investors have direct access to quality online service, loads of market commentary, and real-time stock and mutual fund data. Almost any form of publicly available financial information is available twenty-four hours a day. Charles Schwab started out as a traditional entrepreneur, and he is skillfully evolving into a virtual entrepreneur.

Principle #5: Embrace Electronic Commerce

17. Establish a mobile office.

Virtual entrepreneurs must be mobile road warriors. They must rely on laptop computers, personal digital assistants, pagers, cellular phones, and groupware to stay digitally connected to their strategic partners and customers. Virtual entrepreneurs must also master a suite of business applications, including spreadsheets, databases, and word processing.

18. Launch an E-commerce Web site.

In order to quickly establish both a national and global reach, virtual entrepreneurs are wise to build electronic storefronts on the World Wide Web. These storefronts provide an online approach to showcasing and selling products and services. Being able to quickly and economically offer a retail presence in cyberspace helps to level the playing field with the Fortune 1000 companies.

19. Develop an appealing Web site.

The Web site must be designed to appeal to the targeted market. The Virtual Entrepreneur designed his site to be very appealing to golfers in general, and nighttime golfers in particular. In fact, the Virtual Entrepreneur's ultimate goal is to develop a virtual community of nighttime golfers. Such a "community" helps to lock in and preserve his customer base.

20. Coordinate the virtual and the real-world distribution channels.

Finally, the Virtual Entrepreneur did not want his Web site to be in conflict with his distribution channel of golf professionals. Therefore, he set up a referral system that would link his Web site traffic to the golf professionals' pro shops. This should lead to increased rentals and lessons. The Virtual Entrepreneur's Web site complemented the traditional distribution channels and did not destroy them!

VIRTUAL INTEGRATION:
THE ULTIMATE STRATEGY

When the Virtual Entrepreneur arrived for their final meeting at a suburban golf discount store, he was wearing stylish sunglasses, a cotton knit white golf shirt, beige khaki shorts, and leather sandals. He projected a relaxed yet confident image.

Steve was feeling a little anxious. Now that his lessons were ending, it would be time to put what he'd learned into practice. It was one thing to *talk* about virtual entrepreneurship, but quite another to make a success of it. He knew he would have to approach it with the same determination and creativity that the Virtual Entrepreneur had displayed with Night Vision Sports.

"Steve, have you seen any high-tech golf equipment worth buying?" the Virtual Entrepreneur asked as he examined some extralong Titanium drivers.

"Yes, but I'm going to save my money for your Virtual Golf Shop. It's open seven days a week, twenty-four hours a day, isn't it?" Steve smiled as he expressed his loyalty right off the bat. "Furthermore, your Web site provides digital photos and more in-depth descriptions about the products you're selling." He looked around. "In this physical store, I don't even see a sales clerk on the floor who can answer my questions. And since your overhead is much lower, I can expect to get better prices at your cyber-store."

"You're right!" Then the Virtual Entrepreneur grew more serious. "Steve, I wanted to have this wrap-up meeting for a couple of reasons. First, I think it's important to bring closure to our instructional sessions. I also want to summarize my business model. We've discussed how I used the five principles of successful virtual entrepreneurship, and you've seen first-hand how I'm using E-commerce through my Web site. Now we'll talk more about how it all comes together under a broader umbrella concept called *virtual integration,* as opposed to the old-fashioned model known as *vertical integration.*"

Steve nodded. "Vertical integration is a term I heard from a lot of the MBAs I spoke to before I was lucky enough to get in touch with you."

"That's what business schools are teaching as modern management. But the business model of the future will be *virtual* integration. That's what I've employed with Night Vision Sports. I've brought together a networked organization based on external partners who are treated as if they are inside my company. As you know, I couldn't afford to create every piece of the value chain myself. Instead, I realized I would be better off to leverage both the expertise and the investments of my strategic partners while I focus exclusively on sales, marketing, and business development. I never subscribed to the I-have-to-develop-everything-myself view of business. Instead, I wanted to invest my time and resources into areas where I could quickly and skillfully add value to my customers."

"Your core competencies," Steve said.

"Right." The Virtual Entrepreneur paused to look over a display of sand wedges in the corner of the store. He took some practice swings with a large-flanged wedge before he resumed speaking.

"Retailers with a physical presence have at least one striking advantage over virtual entrepreneurs–they can give customers a thrilling in-store experience. An example of such an experience is our ability to actually touch and swing these high-tech golf clubs. But for customers who want convenience, cost-savings, and a wealth of online product information, Web-based commerce can't be beat."

"I agree." Steve remembered something he'd learned from a leading Internet magazine. "Virtual-reality Internet experiences will be coming with the high-bandwidth Internet communication links that are just around the corner. Someday soon, you might be able to offer your site visitors the ability to play virtual-reality golf. That will close the gap on the experiential factor."

The Virtual Entrepreneur lifted an eyebrow, then grinned. "Thanks for the idea! I want to make a note about your future-oriented perspective." He recorded a few voice notes into a micro-recorder that also served as a key chain.

That's a handy gadget, Steve thought. *I'll have to get one of those!*

"Now let's get back to where we were before my digression!" the Virtual Entrepreneur said. "I'm sure you've seen how virtual integration blurs the traditional roles and boundaries between my strategic partners and my customers. Through electronic commerce, customers will be more in control of ordering their nighttime golfing products on the Web. And through feedback from customers who visit the Virtual Golf Shop, my company can learn more about the products they want."

Steve was hanging onto every word. "So the ultimate purpose of your virtually integrated enterprise is to ensure that the customer is in control, and to make sure that all of your enterprise's efforts are directed at meeting your customers' evolving needs and preferences."

"Absolutely," the Virtual Entrepreneur agreed. "I want to be customer-driven at all costs. And I plan to continuously improve the management of my tightly coordinated network of partners, too. One way to accomplish that is to add a private area on my Web site that will offer a wide range of valuable information to my strategic partners. This Extranet, as I call it, will allow me to build data linkages that let my partners know how they are doing in terms of meeting customers' needs in a fast, efficient, and innovative manner."

Steve nodded thoughtfully as he began seeing the virtual organization in a new light. "In a way, you're becoming an information broker. You're establishing information links with your customers that utilize your Web site, and your network of partners will be given access to an Extranet that allows them to learn about, and then quickly respond to, your customers' needs on a real-time basis." Steve could only shake his head in astonishment. "Speed-to-market, quality, and service should only improve."

"Let's hope so! Another key benefit of capturing all types of customer information on my Web site is that I'll be able to make even finer cuts at customer segmentation. With finer segmentations, I'll be better able to forecast what my customer base is going to need and when. Most importantly, this type of information-driven segmentation will further improve my virtual enterprise's niche focus."

"You're making an extremely important point," said Steve. "Your segmentation strategy gets you closer to your customers, and new sub-niches should ultimately emerge. You will therefore be able to gain a thorough understanding of your customers' needs. And by coordinating the flow of strategic information all the way back to your designers and manufacturers, you're creating design and development databases and methodologies that weren't possible in the past. Again, innovation and speed to market should definitely improve." Steve was amazed at how clearly it was coming together for him. This also helped to instill confidence that he would be able to succeed at his own virtually integrated business.

"Hey, be careful," the Virtual Entrepreneur said with a laugh. "You'll end up knowing this entrepreneurial paradigm better than I do!"

Steve smiled at the compliment. He realized that he had gained a great deal from the Virtual Entrepreneur's lessons. He was definitely going to miss his meetings with such a charismatic and effective mentor.

"By adding a Web site, I actually get to have direct relationships with my customers," the Virtual Entrepreneur said. "This wasn't possible when my only point of contact with the end customer was through my distribution channel–the golf professionals. And these online relationships with customers do create valuable information for all members of my virtually integrated enterprise. My job, in a nutshell, is to turn this information into gold!"

Another question occurred to Steve. "How else do you think your model will evolve in the future?"

The Virtual Entrepreneur grinned. "Wow! You're going to work me hard until the very end! Adding a virtual storefront definitely represents an evolution of my model. However, I think my model will continue to evolve in other ways, too. For one thing, my suppliers and manufacturers will ultimately be able to significantly reduce their inventory levels. That's because I'll be able to use the customer databases to better forecast both the type and the amount of product demand by customer segment, and I'll pass that information on to my partners. Product innovation should also improve, since my designers will be constantly bombarded with customer feedback and ideas. Finally, virtual integration should allow Night Vision Sports to continually meet customer needs faster and more efficiently as our customer information database continues to mature."

Steve nodded thoughtfully. "It seems clear that any successful company will continue to change and grow." Then something else occurred to him. "That also means revising the company's vision statement."

"Right! In the case of Night Vision Sports, it already has. My original vision statement was limited to night vision glasses. I've already expanded it by adding the Web site and virtual storefront with its products and services related to nighttime golf. But the vision statement continues to serve its purpose. Each time I think about adding a new product to Night Vision Sports, I review the purpose and direction of the company as stated in the current vision statement. Then I begin thinking about how to revise the vision statement to encompass the new product. Doing it that way forces me to focus more clearly on exactly how the company will change with the new product, and it helps me to decide whether or not it's a wise move." The Virtual Entrepreneur beamed with enthusiasm. "I'm excited at the potential for growth and improvement!"

As their final meeting was winding down, the Virtual Entrepreneur and Steve Cole moved to the in-store concession stand and ordered diet soft drinks. The large-screen, wall-mounted cable television was tuned to the Golf Channel, which was broadcasting the U.S. Open golf tournament. Tiger Woods was making a charge for the lead.

"I want to thank you for all of your mentoring," Steve said sincerely. "I'm very impressed with your virtual enterprise, and I feel sure that your five principles will be adopted by many aspiring virtualpreneurs. You have definitely provided me with a peak experience."

"Business leaders ultimately gain by giving to others. I'm glad that I had the opportunity to share the secrets of the virtually integrated enterprise with such an enthusiastic student. I sincerely wish you luck in all of your future entrepreneurial endeavors."

Both the Virtual Entrepreneur and Steve Cole stood up and shook hands. Steve remembered the Virtual Entrepreneur's firm handshake from their first meeting.

"Steve, when we first met, you made a promise," the Virtual Entrepreneur said with a smile. "Do you remember?"

Steve nodded. "How could I forget? Someday I'll mentor another aspiring entrepreneur. Believe me, I'm looking forward to that day!"

The Virtual Entrepreneur clapped him on the shoulder. "You'll be a great mentor, Steve."

As they walked through the front door and said goodbye, Steve felt a new, higher level of confidence in himself and his ability to become a successful virtual entrepreneur. Earlier that morning while working out on his treadmill, he'd even had a flash of inspiration about a unique idea that could turn out to be just the niche opportunity he'd been looking for.

He couldn't wait to get started!

EPILOGUE:
GOING VIRTUAL

Steve Cole reached the shady clearing a few minutes before his scheduled meeting with Julia Hernandez. This was the starting point of a popular hiking trail through a grove of California redwoods, and Steve was looking forward to soaking up some of nature's beauty.

This would be his final meeting with Julia. Over the past two weeks, he had met with her several times to tell her about virtual entrepreneurship. Although they had finished the core lessons, Julia had asked to get together one more time to make sure she understood all the principles that would help her become a successful virtual entrepreneur. She had sounded a little nervous when she called.

Steve understood her feelings of anxiety; he'd experienced his own case of the jitters when he finished his lessons with the Virtual Entrepreneur four years ago. But he knew that Julia would succeed at whatever venture she tried. She was a bright, enthusiastic bundle of energy. She'd told Steve that she and her husband planned to start a family someday, and she wanted to get a home-based business launched now while she could devote plenty of time and energy to it.

They had first met in an Internet chat room, just as Steve had met the Virtual Entrepreneur—but this time it was a chat room at the Web site of New Fitness Concepts, Steve's own virtual company. Steve was impressed by Julia's enthusiasm and openness and, just as he'd promised the Virtual Entrepreneur, he offered to become her mentor. She immediately, and gratefully, accepted.

"Hi!"

Steve turned toward the voice and saw Julia coming toward him across the clearing. She was an attractive young woman with olive skin and dark hair tied behind her with a bright green silk scarf. Sharp intelligence gleamed in her brown eyes.

"What a beautiful day for a walk through the forest!" she exclaimed as she reached him.

Steve nodded. "This is one of my favorite places. The trail goes only a short way, and it's a very gradual upward slope. Not much exercise, I'm afraid, but there's a beautiful view at the end."

Julia gave him a quick smile as they began walking down the trail. "I've already had my morning workout, so I can relax and enjoy the scenery."

For a few minutes, neither spoke. Blades of sunlight lanced through the trees and fell like moving, golden coins across the trail. Here and there, red and purple flowers jutted from the lush vegetation alongside the trail, bending and nodding with the breeze.

"Thank you for agreeing to one more meeting," Julia said at last. "I really appreciate all the time you've spent with me over the past two weeks."

"It has been my pleasure," Steve said. "I had a mentor, too. Without his help, New Fitness Concepts never would've gotten off the ground. And don't forget … "

"I know." Julia's teeth flashed in another bright smile. "Someday I'll pass everything you've taught me along to another aspiring entrepreneur."

Steve chuckled as they continued along the trail. Despite Julia's attempt to hide her nervousness, he knew that something was on her mind. And he had a pretty good idea about what it was.

The trail led up over a slight rise, and they were both breathing a little harder by the time they reached the crest and started back down the other side. To their right, a wild and beautiful ravine opened up, dropping steeply to a gurgling stream below.

Meeting with Julia over the past two weeks had reminded Steve about the time he had spent with the Virtual Entrepreneur. The Virtual Entrepreneur had said that one of his greatest challenges was to stay on the cutting edge of technology that could help him be more competitive.

Indeed, much had changed. Nowadays, computer security was enhanced by voiceprints and retina scans. Computers were faster than ever, capable of feats Steve hadn't dreamed of a few years ago. Advanced voice recognition systems allowed for voice-controlled Web browsing, and high-bandwidth communication links had brought about incredible Web-based virtual-reality systems.

Steve and Julia passed between a pair of large California sycamores that bent together to form an archway, then came to a place where sunlight poured into a break in the forest. Beyond, the trees thinned and Steve could see mountain peaks, snow-capped and hazy with distance.

"Wow!" Julia exclaimed breathlessly. "This is beautiful! I can see why you like to come here."

They reached the clearing and continued on to the edge, where cliffs of rock dropped for hundreds of feet before merging into a rugged, forested canyon. The blue line of a river snaked along the canyon floor, the morning sun sparkling in it like glittering jewels.

Finally, Steve said, "Do you want to review some of the principles we talked about? Or did you have some questions about any of the case studies?"

Julia drew a breath and released it in a sigh as she turned to face him. "I have a confession to make, Steve. I don't really need to review what we've talked about. You presented it to me in a clear, interesting way, and the case studies were a big help. Integrating those studies with the five principles of virtual entrepreneurship really brought it home. I know how important it is to identify a niche opportunity and turn it into a guiding vision. I've already taken stock of my core competencies, and I have a firm idea of what I'll be able to contribute to the enterprise. I know it will be a challenge to select the right partners and build winning alliances, but I feel confident about that. And of course, you know I'm a real techno-junkie. You won't find me lagging behind the cutting edge."

He chuckled. "It sounds as if you've got it, Julia! So what's the problem? When you called yesterday, you sounded anxious about something."

"Well... the first step is the one that's bothering me. I haven't the faintest idea of where to look for a niche opportunity. Your Virtual-Trak has been a huge success. I don't think I could ever dream up something like that. How did you do it?"

"I didn't really *do* it," Steve said. "It hit me one day while I was jogging on my treadmill at home. I liked the aerobic workout, but I found it extremely boring. I couldn't believe that anybody really *enjoyed* walking or jogging on a treadmill, so I started thinking about ways to make it more interesting. That led to New Fitness Concepts and our first model, the Virtual-Trak 1000."

"A moment of inspiration," Julia said, a little wistfully. "That must have been exhilarating."

"That, it was," Steve agreed. He remembered how excited he'd been when the "eureka" hit him and he'd seen its enormous potential. He'd spent that entire day and late into the evening refining his idea and working it into a sharply focused vision statement. That vision statement ultimately allowed him to apply the principles he'd learned from the Virtual Entrepreneur to start up New Fitness Concepts, and it had been a phenomenal success.

"I've been trying to think of a unique product that I can use to launch a virtual company," Julia said. "But no matter how hard I try, it isn't working. Nothing's coming!"

Steve paused to watch a red-tailed hawk soar out over the cliff and begin spiraling down toward the forested canyon.

"You don't have to start with something as unique as the Virtual-Trak," he said as the hawk drifted out of sight. "Personal computers had been around for a number of years when Michael Dell set up Dell Computer Corporation. For Dell, it wasn't the product that was unique—it was the way he organized his company with the focus on the customer and production on demand. In one of the classic case studies I gave you, you saw how Ruth Owades founded Calyx & Carolla, a virtual company that found a new way to sell flowers. Owades vastly streamlined the process of getting flowers and plants from the growers to the customers. She certainly didn't invent a new product."

Julia nodded. "Still, that takes a lot of creativity. What if nothing like that comes to me?"

"It will," Steve said with confidence. "Don't work too hard to find your 'eureka.' It'll come to you when you least expect it. The important thing is that you will recognize it when it arrives, just as I recognized the need for the Virtual-Trak. True entrepreneurs don't let good opportunities get away from them, and they're not afraid to take risks that others might pass up. I already know you're the kind of person who seeks opportunities and is willing to do what it takes to make them work. You have the competitive spirit, Julia."

Her eyebrows lifted inquisitively. "Oh, really? How do you know all that?"

He grinned. "You were in that chat room asking questions, weren't you? And they were great questions. You're eager to learn. That much I've seen for myself. You'll find your 'eureka.' When you do, you'll experience the same moment of exhilaration that I did when I first saw my vision of the Virtual-Trak."

She thought about that, then nodded and smiled. "Thanks for the pep talk! I needed that. I'm excited about launching my own virtual business, and I'll keep my eyes open for my 'eureka.'" She turned once more to look out at the hazy canyon. Then she said, "Virtual-Trak end. Julia Hernandez." Her lips continued moving as she gave the password, but it was inaudible to Steve.

She vanished, and Steve stood there alone for a while, gazing at the distant mountains and listening to the murmur of the wind in high branches. He heard a rustling sound behind him and turned as a deer stepped into view across the clearing. For a moment it stood under the drooping boughs of a spruce, peering at him with huge brown eyes that were bright with curiosity. Its head was held high, ears pricked up. Then it turned and loped away into the woods.

"Virtual-Trak end," Steve said at last, with some reluctance. "Steve Cole, four-beta-one-six-alpha."

Darkness descended, and the sounds of the forest faded. When Steve released the VT-3600's handrail and reached up to remove his headset, he found himself standing on the treadmill in his home office. The control pad in front of him was flashing *Stand-by* status.

Steve's "eureka" that day only a few years ago had been very simple: Use virtual reality technology to turn a treadmill workout into an interactive experience. He thought it should be possible to combine a treadmill, a computer, and virtual reality equipment to accomplish his goal. Instead of taking a boring walk on a treadmill, the owner of a Virtual-Trak could turn his daily exercise into a stroll through Paris or Rome or ancient Athens. Or even the mythical city of Atlantis.

Steve founded New Fitness Concepts on the principles given to him by the Virtual Entrepreneur. He defined his niche opportunity and narrowed his focus. He identified his core competencies, he found and recruited partners who could supply the skills and resources he needed, and they worked together as a team to turn his vision statement into reality.

The treadmill manufacturer equipped his best motorless treadmill with automatic elevation capabilities so the front of the treadmill could lift and lower as needed to match changing slopes in the virtual reality terrain. The virtual reality expert had designed a system that would interact with the treadmill, and had hired programmers to develop the virtual reality experiences.

The VT-1000 was a huge success, partly because it put the walker or jogger in control of his experience. Since the treadmill was motorless, its speed was controlled entirely by the person using it. If he saw an interesting sight, he could stop for a closer look. If the virtual path or sidewalk reached a sloping hill, the computer would send the necessary signals and the treadmill would automatically incline or decline as called for by the virtual terrain. Sounds of traffic, birds, people calling to one another, wind sighing through trees, or ocean surf came through the earphones, depending on the virtual experience that had been selected for that workout.

The VT-1000 had been replaced by the VT-1500 and the VT-2000 as virtual reality technology improved. Steve's partners had designed and built the new equipment so it could be attached as an upgrade to earlier Virtual-Trak models. This kept the upgrade costs to a minimum and ensured that a large number of Virtual-Trak owners would choose to replace their older equipment with the latest model. And the customer base for New Fitness Concepts kept growing!

The most profound evolution of Steve's original concept was brought about by high-bandwidth communication links and faster computers. His latest treadmill, the VT-3600, was linked to the Internet and was always online. That made it possible for two or more people to meet at a specified time and place in the virtual world and enjoy virtual experiences together. Sophisticated electronics inside the headsets even detected facial expressions and conveyed them to other participants in the virtual experience. Group walks and virtual marathons were scheduled on Steve's Web site, and many people used their virtual workouts as an opportunity to meet new people.

Although they had virtual meetings a number of times over the past two weeks, Steve and Julia had actually been separated by more than 2,000 miles. She had never left her home in Chicago, and Steve had never left his home in California. Each meeting had been a virtual experience, but both Steve and Julia had felt as if they had spent real face-to-face time together.

Steve glanced at his wristwatch and realized that he had another meeting scheduled in thirty minutes, this time a regular update with his partners. That would give him time for a refreshing shower before stepping into his virtual office.

Steve always enjoyed the meetings with his partners, but he was especially eager for this one because he had something new to discuss with them. He had been thinking about offering college classes as a virtual experience for people using his VT-3600. Initial discussions with a local university had been very promising, and he wanted to tell his partners all about it.

He also wanted to get some feedback from the company's virtual reality expert, who had been looking for ways to bring new sensory elements into the Virtual-Trak experience. Steve was looking forward to the day when he could enjoy the cool breeze on his face and the scent of those red and purple flowers along the trail through the redwoods.

Although Steve was a successful entrepreneur, he didn't want to get so busy on his road to success that he forgot to take time to smell the flowers along the way!

Bibliography

Andrews, K. (1998) Born or bred: What it takes to be an entrepreneur. *Entrepreneurial Edge*, Volume 3, pp. 24 (5).

Brokaw, L. (1993) Twenty-eight steps to a strategic alliance. *Inc. Magazine*, April Issue, Volume 15, Issue 4, pp. 96 (7).

Business Week Editorial Board (1997) The best entrepreneurs. *Business Week*, January 13 Issue, pp. 74 (3).

Byrne, J. (1993) The virtual corporation: The company of the future will be the ultimate in adaptability. *Business Week*, February 8 Issue, pp. 98 (5).

Cravens, D., Shipp, S. & Cravens, K. (1994) Reforming the traditional organization: The mandate for developing networks. *Business Horizons*, July-August Issue, Volume 37, Issue 4, pp. 19 (10).

Crawford, R. (1997) Different strokes. *Boston Magazine*, July Issue, Volume 89, Issue 7, pp. 46 (3).

Dwyer, P., Osterland, A., Capell, K. & Reier, S. (1998) The 21st century stock market: Ready or not, floorless trading systems are here. *Business Week*, August 10 Issue, pp. 66 (5).

Ellsworth, J. (1995) Business on a virtual rush to the virtual mall. *PC Magazine*, February 7 Issue, Volume 14, Issue 3, p. 190.

Franson, P. (1998) *High tech, high hope: Turning your vision of technology into business success.* New York: John Wiley & Sons.

Gibson, W. (1984) *Neuromancer.* New York: Ace Science Fiction.

Goldman, S., Preiss, K. & Nagel, R. (1997) *Agile competitors and virtual organizations: Strategies for enriching the customer.* New York: John Wiley & Sons.

Grenier, R. & Metes, G. (1995) *Going virtual: Moving your organization into the 21st century.* Upper Saddle River, New Jersey: Prentice Hall PTR.

Hagel, J. & Armstrong, A.G. (1997) *Net-gain: Expanding markets through virtual communities.* Boston: Harvard Business School Press.

Hamel, G. & Prahalad, C.K. (1994) *Competing for the future: Breakthrough strategies for seizing control of your industry and creating the markets of tomorrow.* Boston: Harvard Business School Press.

Hawken, P. (1988) *Growing a business.* New York: A Simon & Schuster Fireside Book.

Jones, J.W. (1993) *High-Speed Management: Time-based strategies for managers and organizations.* San Francisco: Jossey-Bass, Inc.

Jones, J.W. (1998) *Virtual HR: Human resources management in the information age.* Menlo Park, California: Crisp Publications.

Liebmann, L. (1998) E-commerce: The payoffs of faith. *Network Magazine,* May Issue, 34-38.

Lipnack, J. & Stamps, J. (1994) *The age of the network.* New York: John Wiley & Sons.

Lipnack, J. & Stamps, J. (1997) *Virtual teams: Reaching across space, time, and organizations with technology.* New York: John Wiley & Sons.

Malone, M. & Davidon, W. (1992) Virtual corporation. *Forbes,* December 7 Issue, Volume 150, Issue 13, pp. 102 (6).

Margaretta, J. (1998) The power of virtual integration: An interview with Dell Computer's Michael Dell. *Harvard Business Review,* March-April Issue, pp. 72-84.

Martin, S. (1996) *Cybercorp: The new business revolution.* New York: Amacon.

McEachern, T. & O'Keefe, B. (1998) *Re-wiring business: Uniting management and the Web.* New York: John Wiley & Sons.

McGarvey, R. (1998) Nothing but net: Creating a Web site is no sweat. Really! *Home Office,* February Issue, pp. 70 (4).

McKenna, R. (1997) *Real time: Preparing for the age of the never satisfied customer.* Boston: Harvard Business School Press.

Nanus, B. (1992) *Visionary leadership.* San Francisco: Jossey-Bass, Inc.

O'Brien, V. (1996) *The fast forward MBA in business.* New York: John Wiley & Sons.

O'Neal, M. (1993) *Just what is an entrepreneur?* *Business Week,* 1993 Enterprise Issue, pp. 104 (4).

Pine, B.J. & Gilmore, J. (1998) Welcome to the experience economy. *Harvard Business Review,* July-August Issue, pp. 97-105.

Reid, R.H. (1997) *Architects of the web: 1,000 days that built the future of business.* New York: John Wiley & Sons.

Resnick, R. (1993) Front porch on the world. *Nation's Business,* September Issue, Volume 81, Issue 9, p. 17.

Ries, A. (1996) *Focus: The future of your company depends on it.* New York: Harper Business.

Rifkin, J. (1996) Civil society in the Information Age: Workerless factories and virtual companies. *The Nation,* February 26 Issue, Volume 262, Issue 8, pp. 11 (5).

Rolnicki, K. (1998) *Managing channels of distribution: The marketing executive's complete guide.* New York: Amacom.

Sarage, C. (1996) *Fifth generation management: Co-creating through virtual enterprising, dynamic teaming, and knowledge networking.* New York: Butterworth-Heinemann.

Schwartz, E.I. (1997) *Webonomics: Nine essential principles for growing your business on the World Wide Web.* New York: Broadway Books.

Semich, J. (1994) Information replaces inventory at the virtual corporation. *Datamation,* July 15 Issue, Volume 40, Issue 14, pp. 37 (4).

Sheridan, J. (1993) A new breed of M.B.A. *Industry Week,* October 4 Issue, pp. 11 (5).

Simons, T. (1995) Virtual reality: Creation of a virtual corporation. *Inc. Magazine,* October Issue, Volume 17, Issue 14, pp. 23 (2).

Welles, E. (1993) Virtual realities. *Inc. Magazine,* August Issue, Volume 15, Issue 8, pp. 50 (8).

Young, J. (1993) Sand, sun, mutual fund. *Forbes,* October 25 Issue, Volume 152, Issue 10. pp. 156 (2).